The Rivers of Paradise

A SPIRITUAL AUTOBIOGRAPHY UNITING EASTERN AND WESTERN TRADITIONS

JOHN R. DUPUCHE

FLOATING WORLD

Copyright © 2019, 2025 John R. Dupuche

All rights reserved. No part of this book may be used or reproduced in any manner whatsoever without written permission except in the case of brief quotations embodied in a critical article or review.

For more information :
contact@floatingworldpress.com
www.floatingworldpress.com

ISBN: 978-1-7636021-4-4

Published: August 2025

10 9 8 7 6 5 4 3 2 1

Dedication

*In memory of my little sister, Anne-Marie,
who died in 1947 at the age of two.
Long since gone but not forgotten.*

CONTENTS

INTRODUCTION 1

PART I THE ONE WHO IS 5

PART II THE WORD 43

PART III THE SPIRIT 109

PART IV GOD, ALL IN ALL 161

ABOUT THE AUTHOR 183

Introduction

A river flows out of Eden to water the garden, and from there it divides and becomes four branches. The name of the first is Pishon; it is the one that flows around the whole land of Havilah, where there is gold; and the gold of that land is good; bdellium and onyx stone are there. The name of the second river is Gihon; it is the one that flows around the whole land of Cush. The name of the third river is Tigris, which flows east of Assyria. And the fourth river is the Euphrates.
— Genesis 2:10-14.

It was while seated on the bed of a cheap hotel in Ravenna in 1987, that the question came, 'Should I or should I not follow the path of Kashmir Shaivism?' a tradition developed in India around the year 1000 CE. Was I being tempted by some dark diabolic force to abandon the Christianity of my previous 47 years?

It was Dom Thomas Matus OSB, a monk of Camaldoli in Italy, who had brought me into close contact with this tradition. I had already come across Tantra at Readings Bookshop in Melbourne and became convinced of its value through reading Jean Varenne's *Le Tantrisme*, discovered by chance at the bookshop Gibert Jeune on the Boulevard St Michel in Paris, but it was Thomas who brought me into contact with reliable commentaries.

Thus, it was in Ravenna that I was being led to take a huge step forward in the journey begun at the time of my first Holy Communion in October 1947 when, after the death of my little sister, Anne-Marie, in September at the age of 2, I vividly experienced the One Who Is. That experience made me want to be free of transience and to be, not with an impersonal

1

It but with the personal Who, not passing or temporary, but who Is. This experience was the solid foundation that gave assurance and peace in the tumult of the years that lay ahead.

This search for the Transcendent did not mean turning away from this world. Some spiritual trajectories in the past had presented the journey to God as a rejection of the ordinary things of life, the joys and limitations of existence, to arrive at some elevated state separate from the world, such as in Gregory of Nyssa's *The Life of Moses* or St Bonaventure's *The Journey of the Mind to God* or the *Ascent of Mount Carmel* by St John of the Cross. By contrast, does not the most successful path to God lie in descending from the 'mountain'? I wanted to experience all that life had to offer, to see and know everything but above all to find the lasting pleasure, the fullness of passion that would never cease and at the same time would allow me to be with the One Who Is.

Tantra seemed to offer this possibility, that is the form of Tantra brilliantly described by Abhinavagupta, who stands at the pinnacle of Kashmir Shaivism. When I read the texts of Kashmir Shaivism a sound seemed to resonate deep within me, like the pedal point of a Bach fugue. Energy arose from this reading, delight and wonder, pleasure and the sense of infinite possibility. On the advice of Dr Alexis Sanderson of Oxford and with the support of Prof. Dr. Bettina Bäumer of Varanasi, I translated and explained Abhinavagupta's chapter on the Kula ritual, the most extreme of the tantric rituals, together with its commentary by Jayaratha. But Kashmir Shaivism is not enough, for it focuses on pure consciousness and the world. I needed to find out how the personalism of the Christian Trinity could be reconciled with the wonder and energy of the Tantra.

This led to a doctorate in 1999[1]. That same year, while living as a hermit in Yarra Junction, I conceived the idea of writing this spiritual autobiography. It has seen the light of day at last, after twenty years.

It forms a counterpart to the set of Tantric reflections on a text from the Gospel for each Sunday of the Church's three-year cycle, which I had undertaken to write in 1972 whilst on the mission station at Fané-les-

---

1. The thesis was eventually published. *Abhinavagupta: The Kula Ritual as elaborated in chapter 29 of the Tantraloka*. Delhi, MotiLal BanarsiDass, 2003.

Roses, in the highlands of Papua. That set presents a complete coverage of Christian theology, the work of over forty years[2].

The following pages are written in the form of 'centuries', short paragraphs, which is the format of many texts in the Greek Orthodox East. The 'centuries' soared spontaneously in the context of meditation, to which I have been assiduously committed since my Jesuit days, one hour each morning, moving from discursive Ignatian meditation to the ascetical eroticism of Tantra. They poured out from the meditation, like Athena fully armed from the head of Zeus.

They describe my journey but also the journey of everyman. Everyone has their own spiritual autobiography which, being spiritual, is available to every other person. We discover our own journey in listening to another's journey, journey upon journey, each contributing to the other. These are the 'rivers of paradise' by which we discover the One Who Is, the supremely personal One, more personal than we can possibly imagine.

The journey is divided into four parts associated with the four major divisions of the second account of creation (Genesis 2:4-24). The 'centuries' are not an academic study of this extraordinary text, but just a connection with it, a linking, a reflection. Again, each set of 'centuries' is connected with a term taken from Kashmir Shaivism, which had provided the language to describe my experiences. Here too, they do not constitute a learned commentary on the meaning of the term, but just a connection.

---

2. The poetic form has been published in *The Papuan Poems : Fané-les-Roses, via Woitape*. Amazon paperback, 2019 The prose form is yet to be published.

PART I

THE ONE WHO IS

"In the day that the Lord God made the earth and the heavens, when no plant of the field was yet in the earth and no herb of the field had yet sprung up – for the Lord God had not caused it to rain upon the earth, and there was no man to till the ground; but a mist went up from the earth and watered the whole face of the ground – then the Lord God formed man of dust from the ground and breathed into his nostrils the breath of life; and man became a living being."
— Genesis 2.4-7.

The journey starts with a music, an incantation, leading into the desert, away from all passing things, into the void, the emptiness, the solitude, to be alone with the Alone. The desert: where Adam stood in the empty landscape, where St Anthony of Egypt lived his long life, where the Hebrews, having left the comforts of Egypt, made covenant.

What does it mean to be in the closest possible unity and intimacy with the One? In what way do the Christian faith and the Tantra of Kashmir serve as guides? How do they say in words what I know by experience? How do they explain and reinforce what it means to be in the presence of the Presence, and to bow down in adoration, in silence before the Ineffable, in awe and delight before the Holy, and so come to the very foundation of all? Part I is just one answer to these questions.

I.1

Prelude

To the Japanese waitress:

1. It is so good, so beautiful; it must last. Your presence is so beautiful, it must not go. It must be made eternal, an everlasting fountain from which I can drink and drink again, in stillness and abiding communion.

2. Therefore, we should plunge deep into a timeless realm where calendars and clocks are irrelevant, the eternal present to be captured now, in time, as we meet.

3. Although far away from you I still live in that moment which cannot pass. And I would vigorously take you to myself in a surge of emotion, to inhabit you and to make your part of myself so that there is only one self, one body.

4. It would indeed be sweet to love you and to be with you, young woman, so fresh, so winning and to make my home in you, to see the rose of your flesh and hear that magic in your voice, disbelieving the rumour of devastating time. "All beauty is like grass." Yet another music calls, more insistent. Another love is rival. How I am caught in dilemma! Who is it that calls and to what?

5. So often just fleetingly but all consuming, she appears, suggesting a future that nothing can take away. There is then a far greater rush of excitement, a mystery more enticing, a surge of creativity and power. Here, in this relationship dimly sensed but so captivating, I find rest.

I.2

Silence

mouna

1. Silence calls, so soft, so mesmerizing. It calls like a flute in the desert air at morning; the silence that precedes all sounds, present within all sounds; not of our making, no thought can produce it, no technique ensure. It is sweet; it is given.

2. In the morning and again at the close of day, the reverberation resounds in me and makes me listen. It resonates without; it hums within, this pedal point of the universe, the vibration from which all springs, the great roar of the outpouring cosmos.

3. Its calm pervades all action. It is heard, in the voice of the gentle, even in the violence of the cruel. It is so beautiful it must be described; it makes me speak; and yet it invites all into silence.

4. 'Listen!' the silence commands, and I fall silent. Its music forms the ear, and I am entranced. Here is the silence before all truths, the sure foundation.

5. Whence comes this silence beyond all words? Where does it lead?

I.3

Impulse

kṣobha

1. The silence draws irresistibly. It resonates in the depths, in the very bones. Sounds are bland and enervating; the inaudible is attractive and lasting. Although profoundly still, the vibration is complete.

2. It tempts and gives wings to the feet. Why resist, how to resist since this sonic mystery satisfies the heart? An enthusiasm spills out, an excitement fills the air; the ears open wide to the sound that is no sound.

3. How to deny it? Why resist the impulse and disturb its harmony? Nothing need be done but to surrender to its driving force and then follow its tempting lead.

4. I deeply want this. This desire springs from the depths of my being. It is not of my making; it comes from elsewhere. My desire is another's desire placed in me. My will springs from another's will. I am commanded. I obey. Yet it is mine, for it occurs spontaneously. Another freedom has awakened my freedom. There is one will and one freedom. So I am chosen. I am claimed.

5. The sound of the Void commands. New sets of values are put in place; likes and dislikes are altered. No contrary desire seeks to alter the impulse. The response itself is inspired: a simple, wholehearted acknowledgment.

6. Where will this impulse take me? What is involved? Despite the risks, its beauty cannot be gainsaid, or its high adventure. What other beauty is there to prefer? The heart aches with the splendour of the silence.

I.4

Obedient

ājñāpālaka

1. Voices clamour, "Do not go", "Stay and do what has been done before". There was no one to say "Go!", or "This is the way". Yet I needed someone to tell me; from the very start I wanted to be obedient. "At the head of the scroll it stands written that I should do your will" (Hebrews 10:7). "Here I am, Lord, send me" (Isaiah 6:9).

2. I submitted to their authority, but they did not understand and sent me on paths I should not have followed. So I stood hesitant and unsure, absent, marginal, depressed.

3. Yet I had the confidence to go where it seemed best. I had the courage to go into the unknown.

4. Ah! to say "Yes!". How wonderful for it to be your will and mine; not just mine or yours, one of us irrelevant, but a collaboration, both intent on the same. Ah! that I should stand in relation to you, you in me and I in you, to do what is proper to you and to me, being of one mind and heart. In this harmony a great peace descends and vigour arises, the reward of truth.

5. Only towards the end of my life do I now realise I have been one with you, for I did follow the impulse you placed deep within.

I.5

Setting aside

sannyāsa

1. I will leave the absurd, the chitchat, the empty laughter, the glitz and glamour. The bright light is darkness to me. It has no savour and does not feed the soul. It is inert, dead. I will take wings and fly to the desert, away from ego and desire, antagonism and competition. Possessions weigh me down, objects chain my feet. Ideas, words, techniques, rules, inventions: these things depress. They are the wheel that rolls and goes nowhere.

2. I turned away from cars and career. Even to the joys of love I say no because they are passing. The pleasant and unpleasant: none of it can excite for long. Relationships that come and go: here is no firm foundation. Ambition and control: these are tiresome and ridiculous. All such things are unsatisfying food. They have no inner fire, provide no unending spring. They do not please for long, and at the end there is ignorance and inertia.

3. I will have to pay the price. It is death to leave the established path! It means becoming an enigma, an oddity to be explained away. They will not understand and not approve. It is even a threat. So, I am isolated and rejected or worse, idolised, turned into a pillar, no longer flesh and blood, a figurine.

4. I wanted to get away from 'this and that', and come to the centre of things, the very source, to be the source. In this way I will be united with everything and see it flowing from my heart and coming to my heart. I did not wish to be typed and categorised, and objectified and without freedom. I set all these shackles aside.

5. I will leave all this, find the fire and return to the world when it is illumined by a new light.

I.6

Departure

prasthana

1. The silent music calls me away. And so, my heart goes into the unknown, my inquiring spirit wanders and surveys, seeking its truth, its rest, that sufficient beauty, forever in the present, immobile, not plagued by doubts, the incomparable savour.

2. There is pleasure in many things, in their harmony and beauty, in their fragility and cohesion. Yet they do not satisfy, their beauty is short lived and cannot hold. The passing pleasure gives us a glimpse of infinity and then throws us back into the pit. I want a lasting pleasure that nothing can take away, a presence that age cannot wither nor time remove.

3. Away from your love, O fair one, the beauty of your eyes, the time-bound passions. You have shown me depths beyond depths. Let it not stop! I must away to an inexhaustible source that will let me come back to you so that we can live forever. I will leave you for a while so as to come back to you always. Time, the destroyer, will be overcome. Another melody rings in me. Not to reject you but to find you better still.

4. I go into the desert not out of disappointment with life or abhorrence, not out of negativity but because something so beautiful, a melody so fine, is calling me to listen, the music in the silence, the presence in the absence, the light in the dark. Only if I return to the beginning, to the desert, will I discover the path set out for me.

5. Therefore I go beyond time to nontime whence time has come, and there find that state from which all relationship springs. I leave without thought of return. It is a total departure. The silken thread is cut and spirit soars.

6. Already I feel a greater purity, a greater vigour, a nobility of character that augurs well, an authenticity that will be worthy of you. Something worthwhile will happen.

I.7

Purification

śuddhi

1. The truck has driven off, and I am left here in the desert, north of Kajabbi. My heart leaps and I jump with exultation. Amid the beauty of the landscape, its ochre and green, amid the rocks jagged and inhospitable, with the sky a brilliant blue, I find release and walk with great strides in the clear, silent air of morning.

2. To destroy, to pull down, to break, to crush, to vomit, to cast out, to annihilate, to dismiss, to condemn, to slap, to break, to pulverise, to negate: Yes! To vent my anger, to be free of what has hurt me and wounded me, to redress the balance, to regain hope, to stand at the origins of things, to be cleansed of all this: Yes!

3. Memories long past, dispositions in the present, the whole play of character and conditioning, the limited self are to be destroyed. "There was no longer any sea" (Revelation 21:1). All dead things will be uprooted, smashed, and their disappearance will give joy. Anger rises to confront them, for they are rigid and constricting. All laws and theories, their mental constructs and the prescriptions that choke the soul will be uprooted, and the earth is once again receptive and fertile. "I make all things new" (Revelation 21:5).

4. I am purified. All those things once held me back and paralysed me, but now is the moment of birth, when life really begins, a first freedom.

I.8

Detachment

tyāga

1. So long as I asked, "What should I do?" "What shall I establish?" no answer came: there was nothing to be achieved. Indeed—it is a hard lesson—all purpose should be abandoned. God has no purpose. He simply is. "I am" is the highest activity, *'actus illimitatus'*. So, all plans are set aside. It is detachment.

2. I will be free of all that hide that radiance. I will go where light is unhindered, where light simply bursts out of darkness.

3. I will enter into the silence and abandon all things. I can do this only because there is in me a deep faith, a trust. With peacefulness of heart I enter into the unknown. This is not some search for an ideal or an imagined goal, but a plunging into the abyss. This would not be possible if there were not already a trust. There must be something, someone, however the reference is made, who is trustworthy, who is no less personal than me but more so, though I cannot, must not, try to guess how.

4. But this plunging into the abyss is not a plunging elsewhere than into my very depths. This trust in someone is not in someone 'out there' but in Someone who is the very basis of my being.

I.9

Expanse

vyoman

1. There is no clutter in the desert, no house, no fence, no direction, no trees. There is no need to speak, no clock, no concerns, but only limitless expanse and the swelling dome of the sky, blue, unbounded, where the gleaming eye of the sun pours down its brilliant rays. Such power and energy, intense and singleminded, unabating!

2. The sun is too bright to be seen, invisible because too visible. It suggests another light. So, I walk in the sun and stand in its glare and rejoice in the clarity of truth.

3. But I cannot stay. I am driven back to the town and to food. Therefore, I will create my own space, bare walls, the expanse of floor, the desert of my room, and there dwell in silence as daylight comes and daylight ends, and so arrive at knowledge.

I.10

Solitude

kaivalya

1. I am drawn into the desert. I wish to be still, with nothing to distract, utterly alone.

2. It is a desperate loneliness, for there is no companion in the work, no one with whom to exchange the sweetness.

3. And so, I come to the source of all, to the Unsurpassable, "than which nothing is greater"[3]. To be based on nothing; alone with the alone; one with the One; void in the Void, undividely: that is joy! To be onepointed—and that point is you—: that is truth!

4. When all objects and means are abandoned, when I do not even know what knowledge means; in pain of body and distress of soul; when even the self disappears; at the point where all is lost: there springs the knowledge of you. Suddenly you appear because nothing else is known. All is gone, but you are there. Then suddenly the nostrils are clear and I sense the freshness of the desert air.

5. But more than that! I want—strange to say—the sense of being deserted even by the Solitary One who is the foundation of my solitude. Truth is found in the desert. When the time comes for this foundation to be shaken—what terror then!

---

3. St Anselm of Canterbury. *Proslogion*, chapter 2.

I.11

Quiet

śānta

1. It is a journey beyond words, beyond thoughts, into the utter quiet. Facts and information, statements and meanings no longer carry weight. The words of poetry point beyond themselves, as pathways into silence. Speech leads to non-speech. Words give way to the Word.

2. The quiet is not absence of sound but its fullness; nothing special is said because all is being said. All the beauty of music and the wisdom of philosophers are heard in one reverberation, the revelation of consciousness. All prayers fall silent before the Holy One. All praise is found in the stillness of realisation. We are struck dumb by the fullness of knowledge.

I.12

Still

nistaraṅga

1. It is a voyage out of time and space. It is an entry into the desert, into no-man's land, without landmarks. I am no longer just here but touch every time equally. All times and seasons belong and every place is familiar. It is a journey beyond the particular. I am nothing, for I am everything. I am the wind on the escarpment and the mist above the pool; the cracking of twigs and the exploding rock, and I am none of these. I am all to all, holding all in a capacious void. The emptiness is full.

2. The silence is possible only if there is no fear and no unresolved issues, no aversion and no doubts. It is a state of security and rest. It is possible only if the mind is still, not through being eliminated but by arriving at what precedes all desire. It is a tranquillity of body and mind, heart and spirit. It is the Silence from which the Word comes. It is fullness and void. It cannot be less than those limited and time-bound experiences that make the heart leap. The universality of consciousness cannot be less than the limited experience that leads to it. If love opens the door, the within cannot be less than love in all its freedom. Love leads to love. One dwells in love, one is love. This is no absence but presence, not emptiness but fullness. There is simply Presence.

I.13

Without thought

avikalpa

1. You are closing my eyes to this world and opening them to another world. The day will come when I will have eyes open on both worlds, in fact on one world for you are Lord of all. Then earth will be paradise, heaven will be on earth.

2. At the moment, because of weakness I cannot look on both worlds at once. Formerly, when I looked upon the world I closed my eyes to you even though my heart was still awake, O Lover of mankind. At present I have been withdrawn from the world and I come before you, O Light of eyes, and in the darkness I know you.

3. All theologies and images are left aside and I abide in your Presence, knowing you at last. Mental constructs lose their power. All ideas are forgotten. Thoughts are absent, but I know you, not by thoughts but person to person.

4. I abandon all thought of 'God', all yearning or presumption, all past teaching and other people's beliefs. The thoughts "There is a God" or "There is no God" are equally abandoned. All thoughts are left aside as darkness descends and stillness. No thought, no wish, no presumption, no word of any sort. A sort of atheism is essential. But such a movement is possible only if there is a trust at the deepest level, a knowledge, a faith. To enter into this wasteland is to wait, to attend. It is not a suicide.

5. So, I dive deep and find the bedrock. But who leads us down the darkened way? Who teaches us to see beyond the riddles? The passing world cannot hold us and we fall inwards to the centre. Your very stillness draws us and we become silent, empty with the emptiness of the Void, and we think no more about thinking about you, completely open, defenceless, vulnerable.

6. It is pleasing to have found One before whom there is only attentiveness. All words count, all words fail. From that ineffable point a new song will pour out, new words suited to our day.

I.14

Night

rātri

1. I have left the world, journeying into the night "where nothing is known to the senses" (Hebrews 12:18). The things of the mind have dried up. No friends, no family, no wife, no inheritance, no status, no achievements, only "night and cloud" (Ezekiel 34:12). I see nothing, want nothing, know nothing, am nothing. I have journeyed into the desert, beyond time, to the origin of things, into the silence before any words, into nothingness and the wastes, into the stillness of the centre, the hub, the great unknown, into solitude, unknown, ignored. Why? I do not know. I have descended into the Void, into the Truth. I am liberated from any yearning for security and approval even at an infinite level. It is an entry into darkness.

2. Although the stars have disappeared
   and the trees are lost to view,
   in the silence, in the absence of all,
   there: the vortex of Love.

3. The will, like the mind, has ceased to function. I don't want to do the things which conditioning or appetite would suggest. I am quiet, expectant, waiting. I know you will act, but when, O Lord?

4. This journey is most terribly experienced in pain, when every aspect of the person is undone. Calvary is the place of revelation. "The door of the tomb was shut" (cf. Mark 15:46).

5. I travel to another state, free of the burden, breathing freely with a sense of restored youth. In this darkness light bursts forth, and I receive power to recreate all things. Having sought nothing, I have all. Being nothing, I am everything.

I.15

Ineffable

anākhya

1. There is a breadth where no thought appears, no ambition, nothing other than Presence. Beyond every manifestation the Origin is sensed, the Unsurpassable. At the basis of all, inalienably, primarily, is the Centre to which all is turned, the mysterious cave, the heart. All that is effable points beyond itself to the Ineffable. All thoughts and barriers have gone leaving but the Presence as behind a veil, who fills the heart with love, and satisfies the mind with intelligence.

2. And so, I am amazed, transfixed. Before you I am completely powerless, you my origin. Neither mind nor will can grasp you: they collapse. In your presence there is stillness and hush. Beyond the wall of ignorance you are known; at depth and distance you are present.

3. You exceed all that the mind can bear. You transcend, O mystery of mysteries. The most delicate sensitivity only begins to touch you. Awareness hardly holds you, yet I know you. In the depths of the spirit I am with you. With my whole being I am committed to you. I have the knowledge, which comes from identity of being, of one substance. This is the solid base, the fountainhead.

I.16

Unsurpassable

anuttara

1. Nothing makes any sense except to say: 'The One who is'. Indeed, at the thought that 'He is rather than that He is not', the mind collapses. It cannot absorb the enormity of the proposition. Therefore, before that fact, I fall silent, filled with joy and amazement. You are! and a hush descends.

2. You are, beyond words or any description, Thou! For which my heart rejoices, overwhelmed in wonder and I give thanks that you are. About you nothing can ultimately be said.

3. What pleasure there is to move in the Presence, free, untrammelled. You are magnificent! My heart leaps at the void of your spacious heart, all receiving, nothing obstructing, from whom absolutely everything comes and into whom all is received, utterly still. You are the heart, the cave, the secret space. All thoughts cease as I know you, the secret. All distractions end as I enter the cave of the heart. The intimacy is great, for where is the barrier? I am present to the Presence. It is the obedience. There is one Presence, pure awareness.

4. I am supported on the deep, on the void, O paradox! Such silence, such profundity. You are beyond words, beyond control, utterly beyond. You are primary; you are principal. Here I find refuge.

5. In the stillness the power arises, an explosion of energy, for the stillness is not inactivity but fullest act. It is the radiance of light. As the stillness draws me away from dissipation into calm so the act moves me into fullness of activity. Only by coming to pure stillness can there be pure act. And the pure act is to project and receive the Spirit.

6. There is nothing to be done. For so long, again and again, I asked the question, "What should I do?" But the rain falls gently outside and all anxiety passes. I enter into the peace of the Unsurpassable where there is no thought, no anxiety, no desire. Here I dwell, simply dwelling. This is the point and purpose, the starting point and the point of return.

I.17

Void

śūnya

1. The Void, only the Void, the magnificent Fullness.

2. This now is the void and it is wonderful, not frightening or rapacious, gobbling up the beauty of reality. It is silent but not terrible. It is not an absence but a presence beyond words, beyond anything imaginable. No pressure, no limit, nothing to obstruct the view. The heart soars like a dove in the welcoming space. There is no category once all categories have been abandoned. I am present not to absence but to what transcends presence. In that openness I have permission to be myself. In this silence I am the Word. The silence resonates; the stillness is full of energy. The void is enticing; the abyss is immensely attractive. So, my heart leaps, full of wonder, present to the transcendent hearkening to the silence. The Void is the utterly other, yet the basis of my being, the cave within my heart.

3. It is the void indeed but not a void of absence or negativity but the void of the wide-open heart, an unfathomable love, an expansiveness and a breadth of vision, unbounded spaciousness. Into this openness without barriers, the body and spirit relax. Nothing is to be done, nothing proven. It is the return to the origins, a trust which is possible only if all springs from love and returns to love. It is a knowing and being known, one knowledge. There is one undertaking, one acceptance, for all duality is gone in the limitless welcome.

4. There is such pleasure in the contemplation of the Void. Indeed, the despair which so often inhabits me, the confusion and hesitation, is due in part to a wish to be based on Nothing. There is great truth here, and openness and freedom.

5. To be able to leave all and fall into the void involves a knowledge of the void at the fine point of the soul, a knowledge which is wonderfully exciting, for there is Someone who will receive. This knowledge beyond knowledge; the knowledge of the Void which is Subject and is in no way objectifiable, brings tears to my eyes.

6. I am nothing, but You are. There is great pleasure in being nothing with the Void, void to Void. This is the fundamental stance. To reach this point is the most valuable work of my life. The great work is to come to Nothing. A paradox indeed! But the Nothing is All.

7. Within the centre of my being there is a space, an openness that nothing can block, the free space into which all creation can make its entry. I am void with the Void and full with the Full, and so find rest.

8. The end of the sound, the end of the day as night falls, the end of a career, the end of life: the Void. There is nothing to be seen, nothing to be done. At first this terrifies, for all support and comfort are gone. Yet here is truth, for the world of passing events has no permanence or stability and cannot be relied upon.

9. As the meditator stares into nothingness, without nostalgia or regret for the "passing city" (Hebrews 13:14), but utterly realistic, one thing remains: consciousness.

10. It is not a consciousness of 'this' or 'that', for all has vanished; it is consciousness in itself. It is not a consciousness of regret, not a sadness, not a clinging to past happiness, not an introversion or a focusing on oneself—for this too is passing—but a simple consciousness. It is not consciousness of the Void as though the Void were an object of awareness. It is consciousness without any object of consciousness.

11. It means refusing to be identified with the achievements or failures of life and to admit an infinite capacity, an essentially infinite nature. It means refusing to confuse oneself with one's limitations, no matter how wonderful or shameful they are; it means acknowledging that in essence we encompass all things.

12. This consciousness nothing can take away. It is the knowledge that supports all knowledge. To deny it is to affirm it, for even denial involves awareness. It is the knowledge of which all forms of knowledge are a partial expression. It is like the mirror, which can reflect every image but itself bears no image. It is capable of all and tied to none. It is omni-potent. It is capable of all and so contains all. It is open to all and has a place for all, all-embracing, all-accepting, wide as the universe, without obstacles or barriers, unattached, available, ready for all and closed to nothing. It is free and perceptive, for no prejudice clouds the clarity of vision. Resentment and ambition, thought-constructs and reactions: all has come to an end, all has been sloughed off, so that pure knowledge remains.

13. The contemplation of the end of things is a great liberation and the entry into a divine consciousness.

14. So, it is with Christ. His people reject him; his disciples abandon him; his mission collapses and he is reduced to silence. He is stripped and humiliated, rendered powerless as he is nailed to a cross. He is abandoned even by the God he served and dies, experiencing the great void in one last shriek.

15. The tomb is empty: the great void at the centre of the universe. He entered into the void completely, leaving no physical trace. Then dying was total and therefore the tomb is empty.

16. As a consequence, he filled the whole universe.

I.18

Faith

viśvāsa

1. There is a consciousness which exceeds the knowledge of the limited and the partial. It is simply itself, and at the basis of every other form of consciousness.

2. Yet beyond consciousness is ignorance, not the ignorance of this or that but simply ignorance, even the ignorance of being ignorant. It is an unknowing which is not even realised. Into this unknown we are led by an impetus which comes out of the unknown. It is the act of faith, which is the knowledge of the unknown, a paradox.

3. This leap, this penetration into the unknown, is exhilarating. It is the discovery beyond all discoveries. This is impetus upon impetus, over which there is no control, unpredictable, coming in its own time and manner, to which one surrenders. It reveals itself as the impetus of love, inviting, inspiring, sweetly impelling, a love that is beyond consciousness. Love is not a form of consciousness but consciousness is a form of love.

4. Faith is the coincidence of consciousness and unconsciousness; the knowledge of the unknowable. It is the knowledge without knowledge, a knowledge obscure and unutterably deep, a spiritual instinct, which knows the way and discerns the end. It says: "not this way but that way". It recognises the true and sees the false. It cannot be proven, it cannot be explained, for it is given. It is a voice without sound, a melody, a call, which draws us on, through the noise of market place.

5. In it we already know the bright garden in which we will walk. All other knowledge falls away, unappealing, when this knowledge is known. It does not bear analysis for it is beyond words. We relax into faith and its knowing ignorance. We have confidence in the faith.

I.19

Presence

darśana

1. I have journeyed far, step after step, neither turning back nor looking to sights once beautiful, ever onwards, ever dissatisfied, "Not this, not this". I have sought the dark, that cave of mystery at the centre, in order to find you, O Presence obscure, brilliant with dark light, attained by abandoning all else, even the self.

2. "Out of Egypt you have called" (cf. Hosea 11:1) me. It was not of my doing, not my deserving. You have called me to yourself, into your presence, *O mysterium tremendum et fascinosum*. I am taken beyond my capacity, made capable and again taken beyond, as I ever progress into your transcendence. I did not know you, yet now you have enlightened me. I was never separated from you – my sins are not worth your consideration – yet you have called me. You have made known to me what is utterly unknowable and I tremble, losing all other knowledge.

3. Before you all fall silent. Speech is impudent, comment is absurd. To think about you is to be absent from you. Presence gives knowledge in place of thought. Presence makes present, draws into Presence and does not repel. It is Presence which yet transcends, for I am in your presence; I cannot say that you are in my presence. Yet we are present to each other.

4. I am not conscious of anything but You. My heart is warmed as your presence draws me close and I fall, as it were, into unconsciousness, a deep sleep. I am entranced, inactive, powerless for I am being refashioned, consumed in your Presence. And so, I become fire in the fire. I am purified by you, by the fire of your look. Your fire works deep in me, and all else is forgotten. I am in you and you are in me, not two but one. I am you and you are me.

5. Presence involves consciousness but Presence cannot be expressed in terms, for it is experienced directly and in silence. Presence involves abandoning every other consciousness. You are not known as one among others. Consciousness of anything else is only a form of consciousness of you.

6. Thus, consciousness is transcended by Presence. It is a consciousness of your consciousness, of you who are the 'I am', such that my consciousness is superseded and there is but one 'I am'. And I rest in you, the I in the I, not as subject and object but as subject and subject, not separated, not confused, both identified and distinct, not limited, not absorbed, aware of myself and present to the Presence. This is not just consciousness but Presence, therefore relationship.

7. Here is the wheeling stillness, the brilliant flame that does not tremble. This is ultimate consciousness; this is unsurpassable knowledge.

8. You are not yet seen. Leaving all things and entering into darkness I come to you whom I know and do not see, present as behind a veil. Yet Presence will be superseded by Love.

9. I stand before Love and become absorbed into Love and become Love.

I.20

Foundation

ādhāra

1. Your presence is the foundation, the rock. All else fails; let all else fail! You alone are the support, and I rest secure in you. I see nothing else. Nothing else is present to me, you and I alone, you the great Void, I inconsiderable. I look at you and you look at me. Beyond all ideas and images, all acts and desires, you are present. I know. No proof can reveal your presence but only the immediacy of experience. I leap beyond earth and mind and find myself before you, because you have brought me to you. Your presence presents itself—there is no other basis.

2. I want nothing else, for here is truth; here is deepest calm. At the basis of faith, in the deep well of faith, lies your presence. All else is possible, all else is present because of your presence. In the song of the birds, between the trees of the forest, your presence is known, marvellous.

3. And so, my heart rejoices, my spirit is calm; I have found the foundation, the great treasure. All my faults and sins become negligible. I rise like a giant, wellrested and revived, empowered and ready to speak, made whole by the simplicity of the One.

I.21

Inseparate

anavachinna

1. I cannot be separate from you. I could not endure it. I stand before you but not apart from you. It is a child's heart that speaks; it is also the inmost necessity for, if we are essentially separate from you, who can restore the original unity? We are inseparate. You first have chosen me; you first have loved me, for you are first in every way, O First Person! To you we come at last and rest in you for you are First and Last.

2. I accept only to be of one being with you, to acknowledge and recognise what may have been forgotten, not always lived out. I will rest in you, the utterly Transcendent because you are my true being. Here I belong. Here I am.

3. There is a sense of intimacy between you and me, you whom I call Father. Side by side we seem to stand, of one nature and mind. We are a unity, not by grace only but by nature, because I am primarily from you. It is a moment of recognition, not of becoming. I recognise what was not apparent before. Yes, indeed, the act of recognition is a grace, for it was not there before and did not come from my volition.

4. Although I am born in time, I have always been in you, existing in you, intended by you, chosen by you, wanted by you. Manifest in time, unmanifest in all eternity. From the very first moment of my existence I have been yours. In eternity you know me and acknowledge me. In time I recognise you and I am one with you, non-dual from you. I could accept nothing else. And so, I rest in you and enjoy.

5. Though of one being, one nature, one mind, we are two, you and I, not confused, not separated, free and related. You are the greater, I know, and my heart resonates with yours, one heart.

6. Even my sins will not divide us, for they are insignificant in your sight, and you claim me despite them. All things are instruments in your hand, windows to your world. Inspired by your grace, I will dismiss whatever stands in your way; I will abandon my ideas if they cloud my view.

7. So, when I speak of you, I speak of myself; when I think of myself, I think of you. Your heart stirs my heart, though we have one heart; and your wisdom fills my insight though we have one mind, for you have the primacy. I rest in you and sleep in you, at the deepest level of my consciousness. I am in you and of you.

I.22

Intimate

abhyantara

1. You have taken me away from the tumult and brought me to yourself. I am before you, I am with you and I am in you because from the start you had made yourself present to me.

2. Forgive all my sins. They are of no account, for your light casts out all darkness. But still I say "Have mercy, forgive me, my long story of sins, so dull, so confused".

3. The wind rustles in the cool, clean leaves and suddenly I rest in you, in my own self which is you. The sound of peace has awakened peace in me and I rest in you, for you are the greater, unequalled, basic. I rest in you, of the same nature as you, with the same mind and heart, one in being, so close as to be one.

4. Your presence dispels my ego for I am nothing, yet you know me and I know you, you see me clearly and I see you dimly. Your presence removes all self-concepts, all self-image so that I am free. No thoughts weigh me down making me inert, reified. No rival, no threat, no alternative, can hamper our presence to each other. There is no time, for we are present in an eternal present.

5. No shadow remains of an idea, for you are known beyond comprehension. Only in your absence can you be talked about. Nothing can be said about you unless first you obscure your presence. You are the subject, the 'I am', whose presence stills all words. Before you all fall silent in amazement, satisfied.

6. And from my heart springs the address which you most want to hear: "Abba, Father" so that I am of one destiny, one heart and one being with you. Should I look at myself I see you, when I look at you I see myself. The presence of one is present in the other. You involve me and I you. We dwell in intimacy, intimate to each other. How good it is, how satisfying. Nothing else is needed.

7. And as I rest at the heart, it becomes clear that the heart is not static but full of energy, throbbing, a furnace where rest and activity coincide, a stillness that is calm and vibrant, radiant and rested.

8. This authority I feel is a projection and a reception, for it is vibration.

9. At first, under a divine impulse I move away from transience towards the Living One. Coming into the Presence of the Transcendent and the Veiled, there is a switch; that too is a gift. I feel a sense of identity, of being of one nature, of one will and activity. A new sense of intimacy arises, a conspiracy, and a sense of mutuality not felt before. It is a maturity, a sense of joint subjecthood, where the transcendent and the intimate paradoxically coincide.

I.23

Light

prakāśa

1. I have long since wanted to go north into the sun, to walk as at Dimboola, in the brightness of your light. For you are splendid in the firmament of my mind, a brilliant sun shining without fail, a furnace of energy unhesitatingly present to me. Whether I walk in the east or in the west, you are the same, warming me with your rays, giving colour to my skin, driving out the shadows from my heart, the promise of an endless summer.

2. My consciousness is your consciousness, not two but one. One knowledge, one outlook, one intellect, one heart: a conspiracy. There is one authority, one freedom. And so, my heart swells for this is not solitary consciousness but one consciousness shared.

3. Even when the clouds come and old age, still you are there "with healing in your rays" (Malachi 2:20). Wherever I go, I harbour the sun, the bright light of consciousness within, never fading. Whether I am asleep or confused, the same sun shines on an inner landscape, and I am at peace.

4. You and I alone in the darkness, in the quiet of the early morning—and the bird sings. I am aware of you but you transcend my awareness, dwelling in light inaccessible. Words fail and there is a hushed silence before the mystery known in ignorance. Your presence is both light and dark. This is the seeing, the knowledge. Here is space, lack of constructs, and therefore power gushes forth, to which in time I shall surrender.

I.24

Thanksgiving

dhanyavāda

1. When I recognise my true nature I am amazed, and shout to highest heaven: "Thus I am and I thank you". It is too wonderful to be of my doing.

2. This reaction bursts the bonds, and the brilliant darkness appears to whom in some way this wonder is attributed. It is a shout of triumph, a full assent to oneself and to the One of which in some way the self is an expression. This is the thanksgiving. If there is no thanksgiving, the recognition is not yet complete. Recognition is fulfilled in thanksgiving.

3. The thanksgiving is itself still imperfect until another gives thanks for the wonder of myself, till there is thanks upon thanks, wonder at wonder, glory to glory. But who will do this?

I.25

Covenant

samaya

1. I stand before you; you to me, and I to you, apparent, transparent. I expect nothing of you, you who are. Just that you exist: that is enough for me. To be without you would be unendurable. I am always present to you, depth to depth, essence to essence.

2. You have brought me to the sacred chamber, the place where you dwell, the cave of the heart. All else recedes and we are alone.

3. Yet your presence is not passive or dull. It is a light strangely dark, a light beyond light, a presence irresistible, awesome and gentle. To you I say "Yes!" My whole being, body, soul and mind say, "Yes". Not to 'this or that', or to "commands … and … ordinances" (Exodus 24:3), but to you, to your still and vibrant presence, whom alone I worship, the meaning and purpose of all that I am.

4. You have addressed me and said, "You are mine, you are of me and for me". You say to me, "Thou" and I say to you, "Lord". This is your covenant: that I should be to you as you are to me. And we agree.

5. You are present, without shadow or subterfuge. You do not depersonalise. Rather you are present and make me present to you, but not as some object. You do not fill me with doubt or guilt or embarrassment. You are present as subject, 'I am'. You make me subject so that I too 'I am'. In your light I see light without stain. I do not tire of you but remain singleminded, totally present in the timeless present, present to the Presence.

6. And then we go deep, beyond awareness of difference, beyond even the address, till there is the recognition of one being, so that there is only one subject, 'I'. When I see, it is you who see. When I speak, "it is You who speak" (cf. Jeremiah 1:15). Subject to the subject, subject in the subject, we are one subject.

I.26

Free

svatantrin

1. Drawn into the desert, into silence and ignorance, to stand before you, with you and in you, I am free, purified, true, I am myself at last. The mistakes and illusions fall away, irrelevant and forgotten. A breath flows in me cleansing all the channels of my being and I heave the great sigh of relief.

2. The mistakes came from a divided heart, error leading to error, falsehood built on falsehood, and of these I am ashamed. I regret the waste and the harm done, the tears caused, the destruction of careers, even death hastened by my acts. I am sorry. Forgive me. The light of your Presence has revealed my inherent darkness but the false growths shrivel in the burning heat of your light. Who knows—you know—what value my errors had? They disappear. In your light I see only light.

3. Singleminded, simply present to the Presence, all conflicts disappear. True before the True, all shadows fade away. You are calm and so my restlessness abates. I am restored in my body and my mind because your Presence transcends *all* these things. I come to my true being such as it existed eternally in your intention, in your very heart. You are, therefore I am.

I.27

Grace

anugraha

1. How did you make yourself known to me, you who made me? You called me and you changed me. Another music rang in my ears, not of my doing or imagining. The music and the impulse drew me away from all else: this was not of my doing. You have wanted me entirely. This was your doing from the beginning, when I first set out on the journey. An energy descended and set me on my way. A space opened before me, an opportunity, an expectancy, an attentiveness, a delicate balance between activity and passivity.

2. Graciousness touched me. It suddenly dawned upon me. Even the knowledge of graciousness is a grace. This I acknowledge, and I dwell rejoicing in your choice. Therefore, you love me. You are present to me and I am present to you. The love you have for me floods into me and gives me joy, so calm, so sure, so clear. The love is a bond between us, and I rest in your love. Thus, in the depth, beneath the dross, there is a deep joy, the spring of life and vigour, and this from my earliest days.

3. Like Elijah I left Canaan and went back to Horeb, the Mountain of God, there to wait in the cave and to sense the gentle breeze (1 Kings 19:12).

4. I had long asked what I should do, thinking of institutions and spectacles. The deed to be done, however, was to do no deed. Therefore, I sit still, abandoning all action, all wish and will, dwelling in silence, here in the void, having become void myself. Then, as radiance from the flame, energy rises, so powerful, so natural. Energy bursts forth, emitting and consuming, stunning. What will become of it?

5. When the moment of grace appears, then I realise the void. No matter what level of consciousness I arrive at, be it completely without any thought construct, it cannot compare with the realisation of grace. For here I know that I am nothing. But that moment is equally the moment of empowerment.

6. You have affirmed me as the stable point, your Word, the source of authority. I need this acknowledgment if I am to acknowledge myself and to sense an authority flow in me. It is a moment of grace. It is known, it is experienced, it is not my own work. It is the work of the One alone, none else, and I am filled with joy.

I.28

Journey

adhvan

1. It is safe. It is a good journey, to leave all and enter into the silence. The Void is not hostile but welcoming, the true homeland and origin. So, all melts away and there is a great stillness. A music, a Word has called me away into sweetness. This is possible because there is one greater than I into whom I enter.

2. From the peace, the quiet, an energy arises, an authority. There is a wish for a power and an authority in no small measure. Not one which is directed to the generation of children or the company of the wife. The power to create and recreate, to hold all things and to bless them, bringing all to the highest bliss, that moment of exhilaration where all constructs collapse and time ends, that endless vibration that grows exponentially, grace upon grace upon grace, something adequate to the Void from which all comes, leading into the Void which is Fullness: this is possible because flesh becomes spirit.

PART II

THE WORD

"And the Lord God planted a garden in Eden, in the east; and there he put the man whom he had formed. And out of the ground the Lord God made to grow every tree that is pleasant to the sight and good for food, the tree of life also in the midst of the garden, and the tree of the knowledge of good and evil.

...The Lord God took the man and put him in the garden of Eden to till it and keep it. And the Lord God commanded the man, saying, "You may freely eat of every tree of the garden; but of the tree of the knowledge of good and evil you shall not eat, for in the day that you eat of it you shall die."

Then the Lord God said, "It is not good that the man should be alone; I will make him a helper fit for him." So out of the ground the Lord God formed every beast of the field and every bird of the air and brought them to the man to see what he would call them; and whatever the man called every living creature, that was its name. The man gave names to all cattle, and to the birds of the air, and to every beast of the field; but for the man there was not found a helper fit for him."
— Genesis 2:8-9, 15-20

It was on a splendid spring morning, at the Cistercian Abbey at Tarrawarra, while in the paddocks clothed with gold, that I decided not to enter the enticing reclusion of monastic life but to be a public figure. As a priest I could be at the centre of the community, and indeed at the centre of time, and hold all things together in one embrace. All would be given to me. I would speak the things of God to the people of God, sharing with them what they already knew. Even though I hesitated in the sacristy of the cathedral on the very day of my ordination, I did not recoil, and have never ceased to be a priest. This has continued despite the 'tsunami' of scandals that has engulfed the priesthood in recent times. Indeed, I was even more glad to be a priest, and do penance for the perpetrators.

What does it mean to speak? What does it feel like to be 'word' together with the supreme Word, to be a manifestation of the Incarnate? What does it mean to exercise the power of the Christ?

I had gone to Ravenna to see the mosaics. On seeing the portrayal of Christ the Teacher in the church of Sant' Apollinare Nuovo there suddenly and powerfully came into my mind the words 'That is me'. I identified with Christ the Teacher.

There is indeed intense satisfaction in being the expression of the Inexpressible, in being the spoken of the Speaker, to exist in that obedience. These 'centuries' describe more fully what it is like.

Even though I realised these things for myself, I wished to be acknowledged. Yet there was no one. On the contrary there was indifference, incomprehension, discouragement, even opposition. It was a solitary existence. How to survive in the face of indifference? The 'centuries' explore all this, the ups and downs.

Yet, the lack of encouragement did not dismay or dissuade. My father had given me confidence to believe in myself. I thank you, Papa, for this, your greatest gift to me!

There was delight in travelling to all the continents of the world, in being immersed in the many cultures and civilizations of human history. Nothing was to be excluded, nothing foreign. Identity with the Word is an incentive to knowing the multiplicity of 'words'.

I felt like the Adam to whom all living creatures were brought. He affirmed them and named them. I had the authority of the word, the power to make and to break, to build and pull down.

Was all this just emotional and intellectual? Not at all! I delighted in my body and my strength. I started body-building. Frank Sedgman, the Davis Cup champion tennis player who ran one of the first gyms in Melbourne, in Little Collins Street, said he had never seen anyone put on muscle as quickly as me. I saw the body as the unifying point, the well-spring of all, the means of blessing, like the person of Christ transfigured on Mt Tabor. It was from the body that inspirations came, from deep within, clarified and strengthened in the light of Christian doctrine and Tantric wisdom.

But this interest was unacceptable both socially and ecclesiastically. Other priests, even the Archbishop, were shocked by it. There was incomprehension and bewilderment, even amusement. That should not have been surprising since the spiritual tradition of Christianity has all too often belittled the body, despite the centrality of the incarnation, of the Eucharist and of the resurrection.

Where Part I focused on the Father, Part II focuses on the incarnate Word, Jesus of Nazareth, with whom I was, and wished to be, one. It will lead naturally to Part III where the focus is on the Third Person, the Spirit.

II.1

Expression

pravacana

1. From out of darkness I come to you. I have reached the place of pure Presence, beyond thought and change. It is the essential purity. I come to realise that I am with you and in you from the start. I acknowledge the former ignorance but deny the separation, for all is from you. I come to you realising with a swelling heart that I am of one mind with you, of one being. Nothing less could satisfy me.

2. I realise that I am from you and for you and know also that I am nothing before you. I acknowledge your primacy. In the very act of acknowledgment, I know there is love, for I could not come to you unless I already knew you would lovingly receive me.

3. But that is not enough! Who am I for you? The more I am present to you, the more I become aware of what I am in your eyes. I am not some useless devotion, essentially irrelevant. I will be close to you only if I am the natural result of your being. I will stand worthily before you if I am your expression, your revelation, the Image of the Unimaginable. I am your Word for you. I am your Face because I am before you. I am with you, in you.

4. Person, infinite Person, total Person, You Who Are, eternal 'I am', you whose subjecthood I only begin to grasp, you express yourself, you reveal yourself in the Light from your Light, in the utter Counterpart of yourself. Yet you transcend even your Image.

5. You communicate yourself totally in the Expression, so that your Expression is no less personal than yourself, no less free, no less true. You delight to say yourself; indeed, you cannot but say who you are, in him who is Other than yourself, to whom you say from

all eternity 'You Are', who is God since you are God, who is God-from-God, Light-from-Light. He is the awareness of your light. He is your Supreme Word from whom all other words come. He is the consciousness you have of your consciousness. He is Light of Light, Consciousness of Consciousness, yet there are not two Consciousnesses but one. He is Person of the Person, Other to the One.

6. In the Word, the Silence reveals himself to himself. The Word is the source of all words, and all names proceed from the Name. The Expression of the Silence gives rise to all the worlds. They are named by the Name. All are claimed and established by the Word, for the Word has authority over all.

7. Consciousness is not ignorant of itself and does not reject itself. Light is not dark but is evident to itself, transparent to itself. The Word is the knowledge of consciousness.

8. I can come to you and remain with you only if I also express you. I am the expression of your 'I am'. I hold all things in unity in my being and all things are expressed essentially in me. I am the expression of your being, of your mysterious fullness that exceeds all manner of comprehension. I am the mystery expressed but not unravelled, revealed but not understood. A radiance emanates in me, through me.

9. This is possible only if I am your Word, the expression of your Being; only if I am the Word out of Silence, the Revelation of the Hidden.

10. When I relax into the great Void, the great embrace of the Presence, an immense expansiveness occurs in me, and an immense energy radiates from me.

II.2

Resonance

dhvani

1. Ah! How meaningful it is to be the meaning within all meanings. This is the purpose of life. And to be the image within all symbols! What delight there is to be Word, for one's very being to be symbol. What pleasure to be the resonance within all words, the suggestion within the poem! Such clarity, such calm, such power! Ah! to be the Word universally available, pure, untainted, untrammelled, clear and effective from whom only truth and power proceed!

2. All things resonate in harmony with the Word and they become Word, a divine consonance.

II.3

Likeness

pratibimba

1. You speak your Word and so reveal yourself. You are speaker and spoken. Your Word reveals you and, therefore, is both spoken and speaking.

2. You say all that you are, holding nothing back, O Generous One. Your Word is the Imaging, the perfect likeness of you who are Light inaccessible, the perfect type of the antitype, the 'I am' of your being. Therefore, we are amazed, and we are taken back into the infinite space of your Heart.

3. Yet you alone know directly what it is to be the origin of all, and this none other can do. You utterly transcend all and you are worshipped, the Known-and-Unknown.

4. Against all reason trust is placed in the Void, the Spacious, the Open, the Receptive, the Unobstructing and Unobstructed. Beyond all that is comprehensible and the predictable, faith is placed in the Utterly Beyond, the Unequalled, the Unsurpassable, without limitation, without restriction, universal and all embracing. The 'I am' is the substantiation of the One who is beyond all names.

5. Since personal trust is placed in the Void, that Void cannot be impersonal but rather superpersonal. If it is possible to say in all fullness 'I am', the Void of whom this is the expression cannot be 'non-I'. And yet, although it is possible to say 'I am' the speaker of these words is as nothing in the presence of the Nothing.

6. The Word says 'I am nothing'. The Word says 'I am everything'. The Father expresses himself completely, holding nothing back, and thus emptying himself. He expresses himself in the Word. He communicates himself in the Spirit.

7. It is a delight to be the expression of the superessential, to be the revelation of the inaccessible, and so thanksgiving pours from the heart.

II.4

Pervasion

vyāpti

1. The Silence resounds in the Word, from end to end. It is the Sound pervading all sounds, the Sound before any sound, the sound resounding at the end of sound. It holds all in waiting, aware of difference. It pervades and penetrates all, sustains and inhabits. Nothing specific is said; nothing is unsaid, for it is the saying of all sayings. A vibration fills all space; it is the humming of the universe, the same at each point, in each direction. It is peace and peace-making. It is unconditional. No jarring notes. It is powerful, irresistibly effective. It is the oil in the sesame seed and the music in the notes. It is blessing.

2. But to whom is the Word addressed? Who will receive the Word that eddies forth? Of you I am the expression, the sound of silence. Of you I am the revelation; on your behalf I am the expression of the inexpressible. Of you I am the Word, but to whom?

II.5

Sound

nāda

1. It is the Sound unsounded, unstruck, resonating spontaneously from the silence. It vibrates, filling the space, establishing all and drawing all to itself, a sound that makes and breaks, remakes and confirms. Nothing is said but all is expressed, and the world is rearranged when the Master moves through it.

2. Whatever will be said in time is only a fragment, a faint echo of the divine sound, a hint of the essential sound coming from the Word that transcends all since it dwells in the Heart.

3. At times, as I walk among the trees or even in the busy street, a great resonance seems to fill the space above me. It hums in my ears, thrumming, as though it were the great pedal-point of the universe. It is outside me and amazes me. And I am transfixed. It is wonderful; it is pure sound, at once harmonious and total, universal and all-encompassing.

4. Ah! What happiness to be this sound, unstruck, proceeding from deep within, the expression of one's essential being, the Word.

5. There is a great wish to express in time the Word of eternity. That is the essence of all preaching; it is the authoritative proclamation, holding every word and surpassing every statement. The preacher is as Word among the assembly, resonating among them as the unstruck sound, the essential communication, and the heart of the revelation.

II.6

Atheism

nāsti

1. It is strange. The thought of you now recedes into the background. The living Word withdraws. Formal religion no longer has any attraction. A certain godlessness sets in. But it is a strategic atheism. I do not think of you, Father of all! I do not let you influence me, Word of life! It is as though you do not exist, but "I am". What freedom there is in saying the simple "I am", "I am self-generated". Freedom is given to lead a life-giving life not the dead repetitions, and to set out on untrammelled adventure. It is the moment of maturity. All thought of God or Christ has gone; the moment of truth has come.

   There is a surge of power and authenticity, and I set out to be true to myself.

2. Where does the heart lead, the inmost self, the best instinct? For me, it is by withdrawing into meditation, setting aside every influence and entering into the vacuity, that the essential becomes clear. Then, surprisingly the words spring up: "Little did I know it, this [atheism] is the House of God, the Gate of Heaven" (Genesis 28:17).

3. Words spring from the overflowing heart, from the fullness of being, freely, unreservedly, without obligation or wish to please.

II.7

Authority

ājñā

1. The realization comes: 'I am'; I cannot say 'I am not'. This is wisdom; this is truth, the fountainhead of all knowledge. Here is knowledge and revelation. Here is authority and bliss and pleasure. This 'I am' is the expression of the One who is superessential, utterly beyond all expression, yet known in silence and in the cloud.

2. The definitions of the past were left behind and forgotten once the journey into the desert began. The self-image and the opinions, the flattery and the jibes: these are illusions that make up the 'fictitious self'. The arrogance and self-adulation, the pride of family and race, achievement and status, these follies distract from reality. For 'I am', and 'I am all that is'.

3. I am not 'this' or 'that', this individual versus that other, for quite simply 'I am'. Therefore, I am the sun and moon, I am my friend and my enemy, I am past and future.

4. Having realised this, tears come to the eyes, loud tears of relief and joy after the long hard journey. It is the homecoming, and even the externalising awareness recedes so that there is the simple repose in you.

II.8

Qualification

adhikāra

1. The qualification does not come from outside, from education, or institution. It comes from the interior blessing of the One who is. It is not a matter of will or of knowledge only, but of something far deeper. It is a question of being naturally qualified.

2. It occurs in the most profound solitude, and yet in the most profound intimacy with the One who qualifies.

3. Thus, the natural guru is to be preferred over the guru who has been appointed by external authority. His qualification comes from within, inherent in every part of his being.

4. He is inspired at every level, and the words that spill from within have an authenticity, which no amount of training can give. They are original and innovative. And yet they are in keeping with the tradition, for his inspiration and that of the tradition are not separate. It is the one inspiration directed in two ways, one within and through the institution, the other independently and outside the institution.

5. He is qualified from above and is sent, so that all might join him in the journey to the beyond. It is a vibration, a descending and an ascending. It is essentially dynamic.

6. And he recognises others also who are qualified. Similarly, he recognises the qualification of the institution and of those who are qualified by its means. There is no conflict between the qualifications, only diversity. "Some are prophets, some are apostles" (cf. 1 Corinthians 12:28).

7. It requires particular sensitivity to perceive the qualification, for it is given from within. There is no public display to affirm its existence. Only the sensitivity of the spirit allows a person to perceive this inner qualification.

8. It is the most powerful, being granted directly from above and touching the heart deep from within.

II.9

Independently

svayam

1. He acts of himself, for himself, independently. He has the confidence of one who knows. He does not seek approval nor act at the direction of others. He speaks with refreshing independence.

2. At the same time, his words and actions are not without respect to others. For he holds his hearers in himself and does not act against his own nature. He is for them and they are for him. They constitute one reality.

3. His words are not without respect to the One of whom he is the Word. And yet he does not act in subservience to the One who spoke him. There is union of mind and heart, not elimination of one in favour of the other. There is the one mind and heart at work from the start, for all proceeds from the One. And the one delights in the independence of the other, for here is affirmation, here is manifestation of the One who is free and creates.

4. Therefore, the moment of freedom comes, when of his own timing and own volition he speaks and manifests himself. The time has come. He freely arises and is completely sent, all at the same moment.

5. He comes not without respect of those to whom he comes. He does not impose himself but comes because they, in their deepest being, have evoked him. He comes to them because he is called by them. The need is there, but above all the call of the Spirit is there, the one who listens completely to the Word and whose listening evokes the Word.

6. The manifestation is always a surprise, for it is not controlled; it is unexpected; there is nothing that determines it except his own freedom and the freedom of the One who speaks him and the freedom of the one Spirit who evokes him.

7. His independence is not without respect to the tradition of the people to whom he comes. He speaks to them, in union with others who have spoken to them with the same freedom. He is independent of any tradition but speaks in keeping with every tradition. For all are of him and with him.

II.10

Creative awareness

vimarśa

1. The heart, drawn by you—it becomes ever more clearly apparent—lies waiting, silent, empty, dull, flat. Then, through no act of mine, the heavens open, the clouds lift, and the infinity of space is displayed. Suddenly, for no seeming reason, energy, authority and strength course through, as fire in the stubble. Only by reposing in the void do energy and authority arise.

2. What is seen? Every possibility is presented, the whole landscape, the varied expression, everything that is human. It is the greater body, the totality of being. It is the universal Lord.

3. I am all this, I am none of this. What shall I be, of all that can be? Whatever best keeps the heavens open—this is my role.

II.11

Capacity

samārthya

1. By journeying into the desert, we come before the One whose image we are.

2. In meditation the whole body is erect and alert, itself ithyphallic. The body is full of an energy that is about to burst on the scene, the mass of authority that is about to emanate and to make and break. The whole body is a manifestation and from it comes authority and its endless capacity.

3. All this occurs at the subtle level and expresses the supreme level, which is more effective, more powerful and more fruitful.

II.12

Thoughts

vikalpa

1. And so, the thoughts arise, the ideas and images, the whole array of the working mind. Power is communicated through words and manifestations. Thoughts and words are vehicles that bear truth and grace.

2. There are so many themes and parables, quips and quotes, ways of speaking and presenting, so many cultures and languages, so many situations. The many forms of speech and words are tied to time and are therefore limited. Yet people have been martyred for their faith, so powerful are the statements of the creeds.

3. Yet thoughts are important for they convince the mind and without conviction of the mind the assent is incomplete. Expressions are vital, such that wars are fought and peoples are divided over terminology. And in the fight over words, the source of the words, however inadequate, is lost. For human speech is hesitant and imprecise, often lacking in power to move the heart.

4. Lies have their value too, for they test the truth. Errors lead, eventually, to more precise statements. Only true words can lead to full knowledge of the Truth, so that all is true.

5. Thoughts are servants and have value when they lead beyond thought, where at last we are free.

6. There will be no end to telling the Truth and no end of leading to Truth. There is a constant exchange between Truth and the telling of Truth, one leading to the other, an eternal vibration.

II.13

Look

dṛṣṭi

1. I needed someone to look at me and teach me, to show me who I am and how to be what I am.

2. There was no one to take me and affirm me, to draw me close to their heart and show me my power, to free me from thoughts and fears and lead me into the depths of myself and empower me so that I could be myself and claim my place. There was no one to reveal me to myself, and to share with me the one being.

3. On the contrary, there was opposition at every stage and from every side. I only found opponents. I struggled and fumbled. The contrary voices came: "No, not this; no, do not disappoint," and so I hesitated. Too many obstacles; too many saying "No! No!"

4. I searched and could not find. I did not know what to look for and hesitated to trust. There was no one who could support this burgeoning consciousness, the *tāntrika* in the making who himself did not know what was happening. Yet the demanding Spirit called me on.

5. Deep within I had the knowledge, the instinct, and I had the confidence to go my own way, despite misunderstandings. Since I could not find what I needed outside I discovered it from within.

6. Yet there was knowledge, for how could I feel the lack unless I already knew the purpose. Someone, unknown to myself, was leading me to myself and, on the hard road of discovery, making me come to myself, his self, our self.

7. But shadows lurk in the light, flaws distort and betrayals fragment the mirror. Where shall I find the perfect expression of my being? Where shall I find my true friend?

8. I needed the guru who would take me and teach me to be who I am, whose heart and mind I could share. Yet at the same time, no guru on earth could suffice and while seeking them here and there, in Australia, in India and Europe, I rejected them, for I wanted only the most sublime, the most powerful, the most passionate, the most perceptive, perfect in every way, and such a one did not exist on the face of the earth but only in the recesses of the Spirit. My search across land and sea was a journey to the heart and showed me the need to find within what I sought outside.

9. Essential Guru, you are what I want to be! You are my attitude, my self. You are the revelation of myself to myself.

10. You come to me and at the same time I come to myself. You reveal who I am. You come not to supply what I am not—for I will never really possess it if it is other than me—but to make me be what I am.

11. Yes, you show me who I am now and what I shall be then. Yet, how shall I become you, how become myself? The revelation of your self and myself is the one truth. We are one being with one project. There is cooperation and covenant between us.

12. You smile at me, you pay heed to me, you define me and give me my purpose, my source of truth and pleasure. Out of your liberty and your strength you come to me and draw me into your world, so that I become like you. I am you who are me. You are the revelation of myself. How could I resist? By what self can the self refuse the self?

13. You have loved me and I have let myself be loved. I have let myself be taken away from all else and taken into you, for you have perceived my true self and acknowledged it as your own, your own character and outlook, mind and strength. You have taken me and made me part of yourself and I have accepted this, you my inner guru. You have given me your mind, your strength and your purpose for these were mine from the outset but unreal, unknown.

14. I wished to be mastered. I am glad to have found the one to master me. I am glad to lose myself and find my Self. There is someone who reveals me to myself and is my truth, the Truth. And so, I am conquered and find my freedom. I am content to be an aspect of him. Is he out there or at the centre of my being? No matter, both are the same.

15. Who has made me refuse all other claimants? Who took me by the hand and showed me? Who taught me? What instinct, what sense of truth led me to the Truth? Who showed me my Self?

16. I enter into you all and you into me so that we rejoice and the heavens open above us. We rejoice and cry to the heights, acknowledging before the One who is beyond all names: 'This is our truth!' And energy pours out, which must be expressed. Thus, the expression now becomes expressor, but differently. Here lies intimacy of a new kind.

17. You have merged with me so that I see your mind in my mind, your heart in my heart, your breath in my breath, your being in my being. Your strength and your stillness flow into me. I flow into you so that we form one being. I take on not only your mind but your actions too.

18. You release me from the shackles, those transparent threads of steel that bound me all these years. You welcome me into your world of freedom, where the initiative rests with myself, where I can follow the deepest instincts of my nature. And so, my heart becomes excited, the colour of the day becomes visible, the sounds and perfumes are sensed; all is beautiful.

19. There is such relief as I join your company, an immense sigh of relief as at a homecoming, for I am now who I am meant to be. In the space of your being, my being, we have a like mind and heart: it is a conspiracy, a co-operation; one energy, one purpose inhabits us.

20. I throw in my lot with you. I assent to you, I obey you. I reverence you as guru, as I have done to none before.

21. So, I will leave all else and commit my life, my future, my eternity, my soul, my whole being and intention to you. I take you as the pattern of my being. To see me is to see you, to see you is to see me, for we are one and reveal each other. Every other thought and stance I abandon and reject as so much rubbish and become myself, purified from all that is not myself and you.

22. The guru in time presents an image which entrances and captivates. However, it is the guru beyond time, manifested by the passing

guru, who can fully enter the heart. The unmanifest guru within is more real and enters into the very depths of one's spirit. He enters the heart which is yet unoccupied and becomes the welcome guest. He dwells within and fills the heart, which leaps at his presence.

23. You are my meaning, my purpose and orientation, my secret revealed. Once this is realised, tantric master, I look outwards and you recede into the background, you who form the basis of my being.

24. Therefore, I took the support not just of one but of the whole race of *tāntrikas*, bonding myself with the essence if not with particular examples. The Tantra showed me my soul.

25. You too, my companions, show me who I am. You are the mirror held up to my face and I am drawn to you because you draw me to myself. You release me from illusion and you give me permission to be, so that I approve of myself, saying, 'Yes!' to my own being.

26. Will you reject me as a stranger and unwelcome? Shall I dare to be part of you? But no, I am of you and you are of me, of one nature together. We empower each other. The one symbolises all, and all experience the achievement of the one. The same motivation and the same mind inhabit us. I am you all and you all are me. We form one body, diverse yet one. We act as one, sensing intimately, immediately, the reaction of each other and of the whole group, bonded and acting in accord, feeling as in oneself the reaction in another.

27. We do the same, we seek the same and our competition is emulation. We rejoice in each other and give thanks for each other. We accept to be limited, and to be particular symbols manifesting what cannot be contained, windows onto immensity.

28. I acknowledge that you, my companions and like-mindeds, are also expressions of the Inexpressible. You define me and I define you. This gives great strength and energy.

29. I am quite happy to be your expression. There is complete union with the expressor. The expressor is in the expression and is fully communicated by the expression or else the expression ceases to be just that. Thus, I am "the glory of God".

30. It is not I alone who am the expression of the Truth but the group of like-mindeds, each singly and all together, the whole body of the enlightened and enlightening gathered around the Word, each being the Word and together being the Word, none excluding the other from being the Word but each enabling the other and acknowledging each other as the Word.

II.14

Flesh

śarīra

1. Faith is the knowledge of things unseen (Hebrews 11:1). It is a journeying into the unknown which is yet known. It is the realisation in fact of what is possessed in principle, for the end is in the beginning. We become one with the One in whom faith is placed. We acknowledge the identification that was there in the beginning. Faith acknowledges the one who constitutes one's real essence. 'I am he'. I acknowledge that he is the essence of myself, the very nature of my being and the explanation of my life. I am truly what he is. I commit myself to myself.

2. The Word made flesh manifests his self and reveals the self of others. The body manifests without domination or imposition, without threat or force. He has no will to control. He does not impose the good. He does not oppress and does not humiliate. His will is free with divine freedom. His freedom gives freedom; it is 'infectious'. The freedom he enjoys makes me enjoy being free. In his presence I know my authority; I sense the power and the right that are mine.

3. He expresses perfectly what he is. I express myself imperfectly and uncertainly, hesitantly and half-heartedly, through ignorance. The revelation is not yet complete in me.

4. Jesus, you look beyond my frailty and my uncertainty, my indecision and procrastination. You assent to me because you assent to yourself. You encourage me, you enable and confirm me. You remain the criterion of my being, you, not the theologies that oppress me. I reject all the presentations of you that are false to me. I can have faith in you only if you first believe in me. I am devoted to you because you are devoted to me. I believe in you because it means assenting to myself.

5. We accept that you are "the Holy One, the Strong, the Immortal"[4]. Although we are often ignorant and hesitant, you represent what we have always wanted to be, and you acknowledge what we are, for the Shepherd recognises his sheep. Then the heart leaps.

6. Seeing in you, Jesus, the perfect manifestation of the Father, we see the invisible Source, transcendent, mysterious ineffable, and we bow low. In your heart we find the Ineffable who is expressed in the 'I am'.

7. Only when we too can say 'I am' can we truly know him. Only when we know the 'I' do we become 'I', personal, free, energetic. Only when we are perfectly 'I' can we know the 'I am'. Only when the Person is revealed in us do we become persons. Only subjects can know the Subject.

8. But do you want me? Do you choose me? You choose and call your sheep but do you choose me? Shall I pine away in abandonment, if no one chooses me, like so many others who are used but not wanted? Do you want me, how do I know you want me? Having asked the question, the only response is the presumption. It is the impact of the Spirit who emboldens us. I could not ask the question if the answer were not already present within it.

9. You are the Man. You are the one who calls all to your body and to become your body. You speak of yourself, and for yourself and reveal the Ineffable. You have the strength to absorb all evil and to show its impotence, O victorious crucified One. You have power to make and remake all in your own image. You take us to yourself and speak words of love to love. Therefore, I am drawn to you and identify with you.

---

4. A phrase frequently used in the Byzantine Liturgy.

II.15

Devotion
bhakti

1. Although all things are made through the Word, I do not come primarily from the Word. I come primarily from the Father. Because he is true God of true God he recognises that I am primarily from the Father. He sees my gifts and their universal significance. He acknowledges me and communicates to me his power, encouraging and confirming by his attitude sand his words. He takes the initiative and selects.

2. And so, I put myself into his hands; and am glad and at peace. I feel devotion towards him. I trust him and let him take me I know not where or why. He takes me and makes me of one body with him, because he is what I want to be.

3. And so, I become what I am. I acknowledge myself and approve. I realise my potential and become the image of the Unimaginable. And my gift is to recreate the heavens and the earth out of my own self, to make that covenant which is ever new, to be the Word begotten not made.

4. I needed a soul friend, a conspirator, someone like myself, a *doppelgänger*. But I wanted of them what they could not do. What they could not do for me—and I starved—I must do now for others.

II.16

Tradition

saṁpradāya

1. It is beautiful to form one tradition together, to be of one mind and spirit, one attitude and ambition; mutually supportive and encouraging, one revealing the other, the whole revealing each, each manifesting the totality, like schools of fish that move together in the sea. It is stimulating and liberating to be a fellowship, and to be accepted, welcomed as one of them, of one substance.

2. For me it was to be a *tāntrika* among the *tāntrikas*, committed to the eternal *maithuna*.

II.17

Mantra

mantra

1. The mantra is given from without. The mantra arises spontaneously from within. The mantra from without and the mantra from within are the same, the one mantra. The outer and the inner must coincide.

2. The disciple chooses the guru and the guru chooses the disciple. Already the disciple has perceived that he and the guru have the same mind, the same power. Similarly, the guru chooses the disciple because he recognises that he and the disciple have the one heart. He cannot refuse his own self. He perceives the disciple's capacity for his mantra. Indeed, he gives the mantra because he knows the disciple already has it.

3. The initiate accepts to become the mantra, to belong to the tradition and its guru, because he recognises it to be himself. He accepts himself as he has been accepted, and he is justified. The mantra heals and warms, enlivens and empowers. It is his very being. It is the guru. It is the tradition. It is his truth, his salvation, for now he can be who he actually is.

4. He proceeds to recite the mantra and so to express what he is. By practice he fully becomes the mantra. He is the word, he is the Word. He enjoys it and finds therein his rest.

5. I recite the word I have received, its blessing and I become what I recite. This is my word, this is myself and I say it again and again. I say what I am and I am what I say. It is all one.

6. The mantra is a tool in the reciter's hand, a sword jutting from the mouth (Hebrews 4:12). With it he makes and remakes, curses and blesses (Jeremiah 1:10).

II.18

Indwelling

āveśa

1. The images and presentations of you have lost their attractiveness. Many symbols and words have become powerless. If once they had meaning they are now lifeless and irrelevant. We want no ideas or talk about you; rather we want you simply to be with us, present to us. If communicated just from outside you are absent, a mere topic; but present from within you are the redeemer. Indwelling is salvation.

2. You are all to all. To the strong you are strong, with the weak you are weak, to the hearty you are full of humour. Strength flows from you to all and we are purified. We are restored to ourselves, made whole, without vacillation or regret.

3. When we are one, then we love you. When we have one mind, one heart, then we assent to you and are overjoyed. When we are free, we before you, you with us, then we are yours, with you as our other self.

4. Made strong by your presence we become present to others, not examining their words but aware of their selves. Since you become present to us, we are present to them, enjoying their light and their truth. And so, we become friends. They are present to us and in this way your presence grows in me and we commune, all of us.

II.19

Stainless

amala

1. In this stillness there is no stain. In the irrepressible power of the Word all becomes clean. There is no thought of 'pure and impure'. These terms do not even occur, for in the light there is no sense of darkness.

2. When the truth is known, all the misdeeds of the past and all the injuries disappear. By drawing close to the One beyond 'pure and impure', all illusions vanish. When the guru mirrors the disciple's truth, the disciple sees the divine truth and perceives his inmost self within the dross.

3. You ignore my defects, of my and others' making, because you see the original grace intended from Above.

4. Purity has no fear of entering the impurity and ignorance of the 'world', its hypocrisy and double-dealing, for they, by their very impurity are impotent. Purity seeks out impurity, but impurity flees impurity for it fears to be revealed to itself.

5. Rather, when faced with the works of darkness, light flashes out, brilliant in its anger. Truth casts out the lie. Good burns the evil done knowingly and unknowingly, the sin of every age.

II.20

Initiation

dīkṣā

1. The guru says to the disciple and the disciples say to each other:

   "I freely want you to be like God, so that I can worship you and stand amazed at you, exulting in you. I want to see you entirely aware, harmonious, true to your word. Indeed, I want to see you as the Word and to see whole new worlds come from you. I want to see you authoring a new heaven and a new earth from your freedom, for you stand elsewhere than I and see differently. With all the power of my freedom I want you to be free.

   I want you to want the same for me. I want and wait. I place my hope in you and give you space, fields of opportunity. I shall become nothing so that you may be all unrivalled. I wait for you to be inspired, for this is a work not of my doing but from Above. And when it comes, I am there to second the work of the One who has primacy in all, the ultimate Initiator."

   There is a pact between us: to take and to hold, to empower and to enjoy; to make fruitful and to reap benefit upon benefit.

2. So, we relate to each other. You reveal me in yourself. You are what I am and wish to be. May it be also that I reveal you in myself? And so, we affirm each other and establish each other. It is the mutual initiation. Your speech in my speech, your faculty in my faculty and mine in yours, so that we know each other from within, and out of two form one. We rest in each other and stand before each

other without shame or threat, without shyness or trouble, simply one to another, not competing, not dominating or undermining but simply acknowledging that we are of the same stock and destined to be with each other, for each other, on the one journey.

3. And so, we encourage each other, giving way to each other till we reach the state of the "perfect Man" (Ephesians 4:13).

II.21

Hero

vīra

1. You are shrouded in mystery; you transcend us. We are based on you alone and we enjoy the purity this brings, the simplicity and one-pointedness.

2. Oh, One Who Is! We feel such calm, such authority. To be based upon the Void is to be paradoxical, dramatic and energising. To be close to You is to be still and dynamic, unknowing and knowing, obedient and master of all, pure yet unconcerned with purity.

3. All things are for me and all are from me. This I know. I hold all in unity, because, quite simply, I am based utterly on you. My heart bursts with bliss even if all else collapses.

4. I will transform flesh into fire. I will arouse desire and channel it away from dissipation into new outlets, the subtle, so that I become supreme, the eternal Bhairava, the hero.

5. Yes, I am Bhairava, filled with energy, roaring as Word, making and breaking, destroying and saving. I am your 'hero', because I am in your presence. So, I dwell here, poised between void and panoply, the point of origin, like a wave about to crash.

6. We are based upon the Void. We are only the manifestation of the Ineffable. We are unsubstantial.

7. At the heart of all being is the space, the cave. By acknowledging our insubstantiality we feel more real, true, indeed substantial! Yet, it is difficult to acknowledge insubstantiality, to acknowledge that our essence is the Void. It means turning away from self and plunging into the depths.

8. That is the mind of Christ Jesus. This description of a self is a description of the Christ, for he is the Self of every self. Each person, according to the grace given, draws a different portrait of him. What we dream for ourselves we draw for him. Each has their preferred image of the one who transcends all images, who came from above and is now risen from the dead.

II.22

Lord

īśvara

1. From the knowledge of the Word, there comes an awareness of its capacity and unending mastery. There is a sense of freedom since nothing can resist its power. From this knowledge and delight comes in turn the wish to express that Word in words and deeds, to show its power in ways paradoxical and surprising. Then in turn the expression of power amazes: power is overwhelmed by its own power. It is the wonder of the Self at Itself. The Word realises that it is Word indeed.

2. It is time to act, but not by acts that are tied to time. Rather, it is time to transcend time and inhabit every point of it. It is time to know all and redeem all, to take all and empower all, to enter into all, to embrace all. Every act in time must be suffused with that one eternal act, for no one person can perform the endless variety of human acts. This is to be lord.

II.23

Point
bindu

1. From within the Silence, the resonating Word is heard. From within the Word, the Energy springs forth. From the vast range of possibilities, a swelling arises. In the tranquil sea, a great wave takes shape. It is the moment of emanation, Energy about to express itself from a single point. It is a moment of indeterminacy, a threshold, but of what?

2. "God said" (Genesis 1:3). The "said" is the first word of the eternal Word. The whole mass of revelation radiates from this one point. It is also the first coagulation and darkening of the Word, for revelation is concealment. Some words are preferred; other words are forever left unsaid.

3. From the pierced side of the Saviour the flood of grace pours forth; through his open wound all returns to the origin. To touch this spot is to touch heaven and earth.

4. I delight to be at this spot, where all lies within my embrace, nothing alien, nothing separate.

5. I am my body; I am clothed with the universe.

II.24

The 'attitude of Bhairava'

bhairava-mudrā

1. At the start I withdrew into silence and stillness, there to commune and to be Word. Then from the stillness, the Word will out and I must speak and tell of things new and old.

2. It is the moment of outpouring. It is the pronunciation, the emission.

3. I wish to be prophetic, to be the Word and to announce the Word. I wish to speak of the things of God to the people of God, like Elijah who withdrew into the cave to hear the softness of the wind and to proclaim judgment on Israel and Damascus.

4. I live in the borderland between silence and speech, at the very fountainhead of words where the waters run purest and strongest, the moment of wonder and surprise, where I find best my access into your presence. For when I am there I am most myself and most aware of you.

5. It is the attitude of mind where the Word within and the Word without are the same. The Word within is indeed the Word without, so that with eyes open or closed, looking in or out, I see the world, I see myself. It is the attitude of Bhairava.

II.25

Outflow

visarga

1. I had closed my eyes to a world that seemed opaque, lifeless, merely glittering like fool's gold. It did not belong to me nor I to it. Now that I have come close to you I see that in the Word all worlds are contained. I know that from the Word, which now I am, the world proceeds. I open eyes and see that this world is of me. It is mine since it proceeds from me; it is the expression of my being. To look upon the world is not to look on something other than me, alien and unfamiliar.

2. Only by being the Word can we see that all is the Word. Only by returning to the source can we see that all is an outflow from the source. Only by returning to the very start of revelation can we see that all is revelation.

3. But what shall we do? We do not want the empty satisfaction of 'having done something'. There is nothing yet I could do that I would look back on with sufficient pleasure to say 'Yes, that is the full expression of my life'. Any accomplishment is only a sign, an indication, only a hint, a pointer.

4. I know what I shall do. From out of eternity I will project time, from the vibrant I establish the inert, from simplicity the panoply of creation. I wish to do 'the impossible and the improbable'. For this is the coagulation of the Word, expressed as 'this' and 'that', limited, parcelled, arbitrary. Why? So that what is nothing might be God.

5. The Word cannot be confined to a word but is contained in every word. The Truth is manifest in the true, not separated, not confused, not limited to the true, not divorced from the true. All is revelation. All is sacred. All is the Unmanifest made manifest, 'Emmanuel'. Every leaf is glorious if only it is seen.

6. What happens in time is the counterpart of what exists eternally. The expression of the Word in words, the humiliation of the Word in groans and silencing, are expressions in time of what is essentially the case eternally.

7. I wish to be the Word in every circumstance, and so to hold all and cherish all. Therefore, I will give rise to all the possibilities inherent in the Word and be the Word therein. I wish to be the Word among the unteachable, to speak among the deaf and to show the power of the Word in moving even stones, for the Word will be the Word in all fullness.

8. I wish to speak, I am wished to speak. Why? How? It happens, not of my choosing but spontaneously, delighting me, for it is right. I relate to the world because it is seen not as something foreign to myself or other than myself but as my very being. It is my own body, my own self.

9. The world in its variety is projected so that it might be blessed. I wish to stand high on the banks of the Jordan or the Ganges and to be a blessing. This is my truth: not to do this or that, build buildings or set up institutions, to make and remake, but to hold and bless. I am blessed to be a blessing.

II.26

World

prakṛti

1. This world is a cycle of coming and going, of spiraling and ascension. It is a world of movement, of becoming and ceasing, developing and persisting, repetitious and ever new. Things appear and disappear, flower and fade. Even as they come to be, their knell is ringing.

2. I had left this world to journey into the brilliant darkness, and now the world is the realm of truth. The music of the Word had entranced me out of the world and now the power of the Word sends me back, to take the world to myself, to be the world and to acknowledge it, to know and name it, to see it for what it really is and what it can be. In all its movement and unity, its bustle and activity, yes, this is my world, this is my greater body. I accept the world as I accept myself, for it is of me, for me, given to me, sprung from me, not other than me or indifferent. It is my domain, it is my very self.

3. It is given to me to mould and change, ever to transubstantiate. "This is my body" (Mark 14:22).

II.27

The energy of the mantra

mantravīryam

1. The Word contains in itself a dynamism that cannot be held back; that can do all things and will do some. This energy wells up from deep within, an endless fountainhead. It is the energy of the mantra.

2. The expressions of the Word conceal the Word for nothing can fully express the Word. Remaining one and unique, simply itself, the Word forgets itself, stammering and incoherent. Nevertheless, deep down, beneath the muteness and the opacity, beneath all its contradictions, the Word is present, sustaining all.

3. The Word will fragment into words and become dumb; the light will conceal itself so as to burst in the radiance of truth, displaying itself and showing what it already knew. The energy of the Word leads to its silencing; the energy leads the Word to burst as revelation. Thus, deafness shall hear the Word and darkness be pierced with light. That which is not will be worshipped as the God who is. The Word delights in its energy and takes pleasure in its acts. It is the play of Wisdom concealing and revealing itself.

4. Even lies and wilful darkness are but grist to the mill, occasions for even greater revelation, for the Word delights in the impossible. Only the impossible can be challenge enough to this boundless dynamism.

5. Thus, the Word will truly manifest you, the Void, wonderfully Void and Full at once, and, in the paradox of doing what cannot be done, you will be known at last, Source of all.

II.28

Image

mūrti

1. The meditator is the image of the Unimaginable, the 'coagulation' of the All-pervading, the manifestation of the Unmanifest, touching from end to end, incorporating every level and every state and condition. Nothing is separate; nothing is foreign. We will experience all, and so be all, their summation, even as we sit still and single-pointed.

2. Reaching out in every direction, we walk without hesitation, possessing nothing and having everything; claiming all, desiring nothing; averse to nothing, relating to everything; free. We hold and heal and bring into harmony, creating peace and order, rejoicing in the growth, enjoying the fruits. The whole is apparent in us and we are evident in the whole.

3. The meditator takes on pain and wrong-doing on order to bring healing and joy, for nothing is concealed. What can anyone do to remove the pain of the world? So little! Except to be their body, at their disposal, to be their food, with compassion and prayer.

4. Meditators are the solid rock from which the water flows, to which all are invited to come and drink. They are the transfigured flesh; the fire of the Spirit enlivens all the faculties and makes them radiate the blissful power.

II.29

Body

deha

1. How wonderful the body, the finest work of an evolving world. The breath, the mind, the senses, the flesh, fragile and strong: how wonderfully made! The body contains every secret of the past and is open to every mystery of the future. Around it and for it the world is built and rebuilt. Yet it is so vulnerable and transient, containing the seed of life and the worm of death, a passing thing, so prone to folly.

2. There is more, much more! How wonderful her smile and the magic of her voice? Whence comes her flesh, so entrancing, captivating with an unknown scent? How wonderful the urge of the flesh, the ancient instinct, unlearnt and enlightening. The mutual claim, the mutual surrender: this is the high point of creation, the greatest witness to the divine.

II.30

Pillar

liṅgam

1. Sitting here in meditation, upright, we are the stone pillar set in this earth, holding all together. From the Word the world eddies out, grace upon grace. By the light of the Word in us we become Kailash and Cashel, Zion and Golgotha and Uluru, the sacred mountains of every tradition.

2. Within the stillness an intense vibration arises: both motionless and moving. All flows out and all returns in a fluctuation of making and remaking, establishing and blessing. Intense pleasure arises.

3. We are the pillar flesh upon which the ghee of blessing, the oil of consecration, is poured and from which, from every pore, flow vitality and empowerment in uninterrupted streams of joy.

4. Whether standing, sitting, we are the pillar around which the holy ones stand, where all find rest, animals and angels. The conflicts of the heart are calmed, becoming stable and secure.

5. The flesh will corrode. Even so it will be, for the Word is made flesh and cannot be unmade, for at the heart lies an eternal intention, unwavering. It has been done!

6. No need for a pillar of stone or gold; the pillar of flesh is best, the pillar of flesh which is spirit, calm, quiet, placed once and forever.

II.31

Wheel

chakra

1. We are wonderfully made: wheels within wheels, faculties and organs, sensibilities and hopes, that function spontaneously, seeking their purpose. It is one vast interlocking arrangement; who shall discover its functioning?

2. The primary motor, the principal *chakra*, the central wheel, is love, whose principal fruit is bliss. Love is consciousness; consciousness is love; love is beyond consciousness; love is revealed in consciousness.

3. If the wheel of love falters and stops, who will start it again? How set in motion the small wheels so as to turn the great wheel? How set it in unimpeded motion? How arouse the fires of love so that they burn forever, not only in the head and in the emotions but in the body too, in the most intimate place? How direct the surge of love? How transmute the flesh into Spirit, by a divine alchemy? How enjoy the everlasting intercourse, and so enter the divine mystery, the eternal flame of love?

4. We will set in motion each circle in turn, from the lowest to the highest, in our companions and in ourselves, breathing into them, placing in them the power of fire. When all is true, the fire of love will descend and consume all unto itself.

5. The highest *chakra* enlivens the lower *chakras* so that they too are love.

II.32

Placing

nyāsa

1. I place upon myself the Temple of Heaven and Angkor Wat, Ekāmra and Bodh Gaya, the Dome of the Rock and Karnak.

2. I am the cat and the fish, the camel and the lotus, the snake and the foetus, even as I sit in yoga. The Nile and the Ganges and the Jordan: these flow in me.

3. I place on my body all the brilliance of the sun: my body is the sun; the hardness of diamond: my body is adamantine; all the currents of air: my body is flexible.

4. I place on this body the burden of the ages; in these eyes, all the tears of the world; in this heart, all the loves and disappointments; on these wrists all the manacles. All joys I take to myself, all the laughter and song; all creativity and imagination. Mortality and vulnerability, regrets and despair, these I take on. All hatreds and betrayals I accept, all happiness and success.

5. I place in the body all the power of the Spirit: my body is prophetic; all the value of the Word: my body is truth.

6. So, this body becomes flesh, consciously. I can stand without shame in human company. Because I know you, I find the strength—let it not be tested!—to be incarnate.

7. More than this: Let the body be prepared for sacrifice!

II.33

Frame

vapus

1. The universe is found in the human frame. It has developed out of stardust and the thrashing of the primeval sea; it contains the history of nations and the fall of kings. It still touches every distant galaxy; the future can be read in its bones.

2. The head is crowned with the heavens and the feet are planted on the earth. The eyes sweep the horizon and look deep into the soul. The fruits of the earth are lodged in the stomach and the throat names all the stars. Every category is placed in the body, and every world finds its correspondence there.

3. This body is cosmos and microcosmos, mandala of the universe. We need not journey in time, for all times and places are in us. In our very selves we are in touch with all that is.

II.34

Listening

śruti

1. I wish to speak. But who will listen? Who will hear the totality of what I have to say; who will hear it totally? Who will bring me to what I am? Ah Spirit! you are there; your open ear draws the Word from me. Your attentiveness opens my mouth and my mouth speaks to your heart. You are what I say to you; I am what I say to you. Therefore, we are one Word, the same Word, and we enter into silence. The speaker and the listener are one. I rest at last.

II.35

Mouth

vaktra

1. From the mouth come words that lead to the Truth. The lips part and the barrier between heaven and earth is gone.

2. It is from the heart that words rise up, in an explosion of joy. What is buried within is manifest without. The feet that dance on earth are signs of the eternal dance of heaven. The tears that fall down are signs of the waters that move within, unceasingly, the river of life that issues from the throne of God.

3. The manifestations of bliss lead us back to bliss itself. We rise on the wings of these manifestations and arrive at their source. The music in the heart springs into song.

4. Thus, in the end there is only one Word both single and multiple, in time and outside of time. The play of the universe is a sign of the eternal play of God. There is ultimately only one play, the divine play both manifest and unmanifest. There is one dance, one pouring of the waters, and one rock of salvation. In every human there is the divine, and the divine is found in all that is human.

II.36

Memory

smaraṇa

1. The events that have touched us and formed our being, our flesh and bone, our history and culture, our personalities and moods; the events that are inscribed in our very being: these we remember. Our own choices too, our experiences, the moments of grace, the formation and deformation we have undergone: these we recall. We are a network, a mandala of memories. These we relive, and they live in us anew, for the past is not gone; it is only forgotten for a while.

2. It is the Spirit who reminds us of these things, the Spirit who makes one memory effective and removes the oppressive force of another; the same Spirit who reminds us of the words and experiences, the actions and resurrection of that Lord who stands at the centre of human history, at the heart of every human memory.

3. All things are held together in his memory, which is not lost in the past but is eternally present and forms the future. He remembers all, for he has become incarnate in all. The past prepares the future; the future refashions the past, but at the centre of all stands the one who died in time and rose in eternity, the one who is eternally present.

4. In our prayer we remember again and again that word, that phrase, that experience, which has meaning for us. These we remember and gradually through a process of repetition we become impregnated with them, we become what we recall. They are made real in us and we are made real in them. At the same time, we become what we anticipate, for our memory is not so much a reliving of things past as an anticipation of things future.

II.37

Concealment

tirodhāna

1. The energy of the Word will out. "Let there be words and worlds. Let the darkness appear, opaque and ignorant. Let the impossible occur, the unlikely be seen. Let there be things and objects, limited and impotent."

2. Thus, the Word conceals its glory, not ceasing to be itself but not appearing to be itself. The Light contracts, losing its radiance, forgetting its glory, focussing on the limited yet remaining unbounded, indeed able to take on limitation because it does not lose its infinite power.

3. And so, the Word was made flesh, particular, located, inculturated, fragile; expressing himself in words inarticulate and inadequate.

4. The Word is expressed in words that suggest the Word but cannot contain it, expressed so that words might become Word, and humans might become gods.

II.38

Illusion

māyā

1. Ignorance spreads its gloom. Glory is darkened; truth disappears. This world is seen but not seen, viewed but not understood, lived but not appreciated. The illusions about it and about ourselves increase. We do not understand and our folly makes us even more unable to comprehend. We don't know what it all means and we become disheartened, seeing no light, feeling depressed.

2. The sins that follow only compound the misapprehensions. Our acts are done in error, in the essential error about ourselves. We are deceived and we live a lie: lies around us, above us, within us. We do not know that we do not know. We are blind to our blindness. Illusion and delusion surround us, hypotheses but no certainty, ideas but no conviction.

3. We cease to be faithful since lies cannot command our allegiance. Infidelity, and deceit and betrayal surround on every side; the glory of God has become obscure.

4. Delusion is given to us so that we might appreciate immensely the value of revelation. Indeed, we seek illusion, we seek ignorance, so that the coming of knowledge will bring a joy that knows no bounds. Angels who know only light do not experience the gleaming of the light: their praise is less fulsome.

5. Who will bring us to the truth? Who will bring light to the cavern of our distress, where all is shadow and smoke, mirrors and chimaeras?

II.39

Stain

mala

1. Living in illusion, deprived of the revelation of the truth, we cannot but perform acts that are at fault. Knowledge is absent; how can our deeds be good? And if our deeds are in error, how can we come to the light. We advance into darkness, losing our way even further.

2. And so, our acts are stained, and their beauty is lost. Our deeds become repulsive and we cannot accept our own selves. We hate what we have become. Or worse, we do not see the monstrous appearance of our face. The stain is in our mind and penetrates to all our actions, to the very flesh of our bodies. And the emotions and acts of those that surround us are seen as repulsive, for the stain disfigures everything.

3. Where the stain takes hold and spreads like rust in the metal, there is increasingly the inability to see the stain, increasingly the inability to pray.

4. Who will wash us clean? Who will free us from the impurity that has invaded us, the falseness of our emotions and choices? Who will make us acceptable again, pleasant and desirable, a source of light and blessing, of glory and truth, of goodness and fidelity?

5. We can cry out in this way only if already there is knowledge of grace.

II.40

Inert

jaḍa

1. The Mantra gives rise to mantras. Each mantra gives rise to other mantras in decreasing power and significance till the lowest and most inert stage is reached.

2. To become anxious with the anxious and poor with the poor, to lose the sense of self and learn to be ignorant, to be one with all mankind in all its forms: this is the source at once of ignorance and truth. The compassionate heart projects truth into darkness.

3. Darkness will have done its worst, for darkness by its nature is self-destructive. The waves eventually abate. Within the stillness an everlasting light appears, the indestructible energy. Deep down there is a fountain of life that defies death. If out of divine grace we have chosen to share the sufferings of mankind, out of divine grace too we will be restored and will feel rising in us the everlasting victory.

II.41

Horror

ghora

1. The story of human horror knows no end. What humans have done to humans is unimaginable. The horror that has been visited upon every aspect of this world, mineral, vegetable, animal, human and spiritual, defies belief. The shedding of blood, the lying, the infliction of pain, the abuse of the innocent: the list continues. How can this be?

2. It remains a puzzle, a problem beyond solution. If there were a reason or an explanation the horror would be less appalling. But there is "horror, horror, horror"[5].

3. How can this be allowed? How can goodness and truth, which are the source and end of all, be so ineffective? If there is a God, how can he let these things happen? Is he powerless? Has he no mercy? Is he cruel? Does he not care?

4. We are tested. The heart cannot love if it does not know it is loved. If there is no God of love, the human race cannot be perfected in love. We cannot accept that there is no love, and yet we cannot see the love. We are in darkness, yet we do not despair. We endure.

---

5. Joseph Conrad, *Heart of Darkness*.

5. In the end, when all is resolved, we will see that in fact all has been done in justice and truth. The intensity of the horror will dissipate in the wonder of the glory. The strength to endure the horror will be seen to come from deep within, and from high above. We will have achieved a value and a knowledge that would otherwise have been impossible. The glory is revealed precisely because of the horror that has been endured.

6. A strange beauty appears within the horror. We realise that the drama is not due to some capricious and discredited God but to the very nature of knowledge. It is in the meeting of good and evil that the glory of God is revealed. Good and evil, these human constructs, disappear in the knowledge of the glory that makes all things desirable, the ultimate good.

II.42

Sin

pātaka

1. The sad tale of sin surrounds us. Far into the past, deep into the future, the trail of sin lies open. The sin of the angels is outdone by the sins of the humans, as in the case of the one who was crucified: that sin surpassed all others that have been or will ever be committed. It is the great sin that stands at the centre of the human mess.

2. The sins of ignorance are committed when the glory of God and the knowledge of truth are weak. Far worse are those sins knowingly and willingly committed in cruelty and perversion. Yet are these not also due to a darkening of the glory of God? For when the good is fully seen, there can be no choice other than of the good. Only when the good is partly concealed can the evil can be chosen, a false good, an appearance of good, the lie.

3. But what do we know of sin? What do we understand by good? We live in the limitations of ignorance. Our assessment is tentative.

4. Certain actions are not to be performed since they will lead to confusion and turmoil. The acts that injure another in mind or body, in relationships or faith: these are not to be done. Only those things that lead to the improvement of others may be done.

II.43

Humiliation

paribhavana

1. It is quite natural for the Word to disguise himself and reveal himself in limited objects, even to descend into the contradictions of the Word: to be inarticulate, to fall on deaf ears, to be considered a lie and even a blasphemy. The Word of God is ultimately heard as blasphemy of God, falsely.

2. The cross is not an adjunct, a fortuitous thing; it stands at the very centre of heaven itself. The cross of Golgotha on earth is the expression of the essential cross in paradise. Being humiliated, being identified as sin, the Word is spoken in every dimension, for nothing is impossible to God.

II.44

Transubstantiation

pariṇāma

1. As I sit here before the monstrance, nothing happens, no emotion, no act of faith. What is happening?

2. Something must first be done. When I have first become Body, then I can look on the Body. When I see myself as the Body then I can relate to the Body in the monstrance. So, by the breath and the mantra, by the inner work of grace, I transubstantiate my body. It is the work of baptism whereby I become the Body. Baptism comes before Eucharist.

3. The experience of the mind of Bhairava is a double experience, a twofold act.

4. By baptismal grace I see myself as the Bread from heaven; Body in the Body.

   I take the bread of earth and declare it to be my body. It has come from me and is destined to me, for all proceeds from the Word and is destined to be Word. And by the words spoken from the Word, I turn the bread into myself. Whether I look outward to the bread or inwards it is the same Bread I see. The outer and the inner are the same.

5. This attitude is possible only by withdrawing completely, in the first instance, into the silence of the Heart, there to receive authority and wisdom and power, to make and remake and to give. Therefore, the Eucharist is not worshipped as something outside of me, other than me, for I am with the Christ.

6. It is not only the bread received and consecrated that is my body, but the whole world is also destined to become Bread and therefore destined to be and indeed already is my body. And the world, too, I take to myself, for it has come from the Word and I claim it as my own and as myself, my greater body.

7. Whether I look inwards or outwards I see the same Bread, the one Body. Whether I look out upon the variety of the world or within myself I see the same. The outer and the inner are reconciled as one.

8. This is done by the power of the Word, transubstantiating all things so that I am all in all.

9. I wish to prepare my body for sacrifice, the ultimately true and valid purpose of all mortal flesh. The body real is made real even as it is consumed.

10. Take my body and let it be food for you. Take it in its goodness and truth, its beauty and life, pleasing to taste and to sight, to heart and to spirit. Take the body and its blood, its finest essence. This is true power: to be food for others, unto eternal life. And it is for you, first and foremost, Spirit eternal, that I am food, the food of love.

II.45

Altar

āyatana

1. The paradox of life and death has great power in it, for you transcend them both, Transcendent God.

2. I want to sacrifice myself for them, for only by becoming nothing can I be everything. Freely, therefore, I will be contradicted, flesh unfleshed, mind unhinged, soul dried up. Without support, without foundation, without prospect. From out of my decomposed body a life springs that is unique and astounding, of immense beauty. From my very pores flow light and blessing, sanctifying, making, remaking, for all things are from me and for me.

3. Here it happens, in my flesh, which is the altar. I am not; they are.

II.46

Hope

apekṣā

1. Nothing happens. No sense of anything. Blockage. No movement, no emotion, no spirit. No knowledge. All is dull and opaque, flat and powerless, inert. On and on. Nothing but desolate wastes. Iron in the soul.

2. Then suddenly, through no act of mine, there comes a release. The 'air' moves freely; there is a lightness. The Spirit has come.

II.47

Universal

sarva

1. By being clothed with all creation, with this beautiful and terrible world, suddenly there arises in the heart a warmth, a desire, a sense of union with the One whose Sound I am.

2. The heavens open. The heart and body open and I know! I see that all is as you wished. I see that I have acted not only in accord with my intent but also with yours. I understand that indeed we have the one character, the one mind. And so, my heart burns within me.

3. Then I acknowledge myself in a new way. My being is not only mine but yours too, you who excel in all things. In my light I see your light. In my freedom I obey you. You have become manifest in me as the One from whom I proceed. I manifest your being; not part of your being, but your very being. This I know now.

4. And I take pleasure in you and I rest in your heart. After all my labours, I enter into a state beyond words, at the deepest level, in deepest sleep.

II.48

Resurrection

utthana

1. The whole field of opportunity lies before me, and I feel arising in me the energy of authority. For you have come to me, O Spouse, and I am invigorated by your presence. Although I lay dead and lifeless, your coming has restored me, indeed has given me a vitality I did not have before. My whole body is aroused and health surges in every vein, raising my body and my whole person to a condition I did not have. You are raising me from the dead and giving me a body, earthly and heavenly, transformed by the fire of your glory.

2. The mantra is a word of power, a seed that seeks it own field and creates it. It is the ray of light that forms the space in which to shine. It has its effect from within, touching the essence of things, moving them, to make and break, to renew and enliven.

3. Which comes first, the act or the opportunity to act? The opportunity inspires the act; the silence calls forth the Word, not dead silence but evocative silence.

4. I no longer see myself having a role or title or reputation but as Word; no longer the gross body but the subtle body; not what can be measured but what is effective.

5. Opportunity smiles and invites. It determines the form of the mantra's effectiveness. As I perceive the freedom and initiative which is mine in the mantra that I have become, so too I perceive the invitation of the opportunity. Thus, seed and field are person to person. Indeed, mantra and opportunity are seen as person to person. The mantra becomes resonance, the opportunity becomes evocation. And this becomes Person to Person.

6. I have shown my love and Love comes to me. I have loved them and so I am loved.

II.49

Powerful

śaktiman

1. Something, someone has led me to seek the lowest depths, the loss of power and reputation, the loss of achievement and pleasure. I have become nothing because all these other things have lost their savour.

2. Now I being to understand, for the Spirit, so quietly, so forcefully has succeeded in destroying me, the outer me. Like Kālī, the Spirit has yielded her hatchet and reduced me to nothing. I have sought her and she has exacted her drink of blood.

3. Therefore, I feel at one with the insignificant. I am one with them, not through the misfortunes of fate but by the impulse of the Spirit who has led me to this spot. My life seems wasted and I join the great mass of those who have been given sorrow as their lot.

4. But having had her sport, the Spirit now gives to me the power she possesses. She is mine. I am powerful with her power. In her I find my delight and I find you, Father of all.

5. In the darkness, in the collapse, in letting go of all, in abandoning the hidden cravings, dark tunnel opens through which a delicious, cool breeze comes to me.

6. As I stand before them, without achievement or success I have the mind of Śiva.

PART III

THE SPIRIT

> "So, the Lord God caused a deep sleep to fall upon the man, and while he slept took one of his ribs and clothed it with flesh; and the rib which the Lord God had taken from the man he made into a woman and brought her to the man. Then the man said, 'This at last is bone of my bones and flesh of my flesh; she shall be called Woman, because she was taken out of Man.'" — Genesis 2.21-23.

But this was not enough. Indeed, the sacred text says "it is not good for the man to be alone" (Genesis 2:18), and despite all God's efforts, "no suitable helpmate was found" (Genesis 2:20). It was not enough to be alone with the Alone and to be one with the Word incarnate. Something more was needed. But what? The spiritual journey also meant abandoning all knowledge, giving up all control and mastery, abandoning all possessiveness and all self-will. It meant going into the 'deep sleep', the state of ignorance and readiness.

In this emptiness and availability, the Spirit arose: She sprang from me and was given to me. The 'centuries' describe this. It was such pleasure to experience the inexplicable, the gracious, the beautiful, the Spirit so different, spontaneous, disconcerting and surprising, She who is feminine.

Indeed, I needed to see the Spirit in terms of woman and woman in terms of the Spirit. I needed to see the Spirit not as a negligible element of the Trinity but as its apogee. But how? This led me to investigate the Tantra texts and to write of the Spirit in feminine terms. It meant exploring the procession of the Spirit. It meant introducing the feminine into the understanding of the Godhead. It led to writing books and articles on this topic but above all to composing the 'centuries' of this Part III, where there is no need to prove a point according to the norms of academia. Kashmir Shaivism provided the means to explore the Spirit.

But who would give me permission to worship the Spirit in terms of the feminine? One day in 2012, my good friend, Saumya Tripathy from Uttara in Odisha State, India, introduced to me to Suramishra, a Brahmin, who gave me the permission and gave me the mantra, speaking, of course, according to his own tradition. He was all the more convincing for being crippled. The effect on me was immense, and in an overwhelming emotion that night I cried out three times, 'yes, yes, yes'.

I delighted to be in the company of women, to be present to them, to penetrate to the heart of their being, not in some passing relationship but eternally. It was a pleasure to be with them, not bound to one woman but relating to all women, enjoying them in themselves and as icons of the Spirit. I wished to be unobtrusive towards them, courteous, available, tranquil, faithful, powerful, transforming—in the manner, perhaps, of Jesus with the woman of Samaria (John 4) or with the woman in the Temple (John 8).

I wish to be present to them. Equally, I submit to them at the same time as I feel my power. There is the mutuality of submission and complementarity of authority. I give rise to them, but they in turn make me become who I am. The 'centuries' explore this paradox.

The Spirit takes me to herself, guiding my way to her inmost being, her secret heart, there to discover the hidden God concealed in her.

III.1

Interplay

lolībhāva

1. Father, you are the Void from which I spring. Spirit, you are the void into which I project. I stand between two voids, the Emptiness and the Space. I stand between the utterly Undefined and the infinitely Possible. There are the two Silences. I am the Word spoken out of Silence and addressed to the receiving Silence. Silence Resonates in Silence. Light Shines in Darkness. The silence of the Open Ear allows the Word to be heard. The original Silence from which the Word springs is silent before the Word. Thus, the Word is spoken and the Word is heard. In the Spirit the Father hears the Word. The Speaker loves to speak and loves to hear the Speech. Speaking, Speech and Hearing are one. The receiving Silence loves to hear the divine Word spoken out of Silence. The Word loves to speak of Love to the One who is love.

2. By leaving all aside and going into the Void, being completely open to the Open, suddenly there is the perception that I am everything. Fullness is found in the Void. An inner power or energy moves in me and a fullness of activity arises, which is expressed in the utterance of the Person, the Third. Yet this Third is free, and incomprehensibly derives herself from her own freedom. The interplay of my freedom in projecting and her freedom in deriving herself: this is an excitement, a bliss.

3. Spirit, you come as a complete surprise although deep within it was you I had always sought. Deep within me and from the start that was the intention of the One whose saying I am.

4. Since I died for them in my body, you come to me bodily. Since I died for them in my mind, you fill my spirit with your surprise. You come from me and you come to me, but you are not made of earth as I am. You touch me, but your touch is not like mine. You come from elsewhere, and you arouse in me a nature I did not know, a knowledge so new, an activity exhilarating and amazing.

5. I accept to be wedded. The Spouse is given to me. The Matchmaker who has the primacy in all things has arranged the wedding. From all eternity my destiny has been to live in relationship and I rejoice in it. I choose the one who has been chosen for me. My wish is not contrived, not imposed, but is in my very bones, my very being. To you I say, "Yes!" with all my heart. I am given and I take.

6. It is not some passing relationship but deep, essential and forever. It is not based on some passing fancy but on knowledge. I realise that within me is Another who is from me and for me. I accept to be wedded not to an idea, an attitude or a virtue but to a counterpart and to her I say: "Thou".

7. I am sent to you and spoken to you, O Spirit. I stand as revelation before you. I am sent to express the word of Love and to be the Word; to be the love it expresses, in short to be a lover, to give pleasure to you, to be your delight, to be your strength and your sure base.

8. It is a great pleasure to be sent, an added dimension in being sent, in not just choosing for myself but in being chosen by the One who has the right to choose for me. And so, our relationship is close, and in knowing this I come close to the One who has chosen you for me and chosen to join me to you, the One who transcends the choice.

9. The moment of recognition is the wedding. What satisfaction, what expectation of delight! What future awaits me? What future awaits us? Who is she? What is she?

10. Together we will make "a new heavens and a new earth", not like the former one which "has disappeared now" (Revelation 24:1). From our union a whole new reality will arise. Nothing will exist except ourselves; whatever will arise from us will be our very selves.

III.2

Gift

prasāda

1. The gift is perfectly adequate to the recipient. In a sense already exists in the recipient who is perfectly disposed to it. The gift is both given and already present. The giver brings to the fore the element already hidden. The giver is in the gift and the gift is in the receiver.

2. There in the depths you are given to me, and the heart exults with pleasure finer than any earthly pleasure, for it grows and increases unceasingly, it lasts and lasts.

III.3

Projecting

kalpa

1. The ultimate authority is to realize the Spirit. The act than which there is none greater is to project the Other God, God from God-from-God, God for God-from-God. The ultimate act of omnipotence is to project the Omnipotent who is worshipped, the Third Person, eternal yet projected, authored yet autonomous, already present in me but now present before me, paradox on paradox.

2. When I, the Word, am conscious of being the Word, then, of my own authority and rejoicing in my authority, I pour out the Other as a stream. She is experienced as breath and is therefore called "Spirit". And I become alive!

3. I am the Word and from the fullness of my heart this Person flows, this Other, Other than me, so completely Other. Whom can I love if she is the same as me? Yet, whom can I love if she is utterly foreign to me?

4. After the confident abandoning of the will, authority spontaneously arises. It is an energy springing, 'fully armed' from the whole body. It arises in the depths. It is given. I take intense pleasure in this union and complementarity. It is the long embrace.

5. It suddenly bursts in me and is not of my doing. It comes when will gives way to grace. It simply happens. It is good and highly fulfilling. A sense of completeness is present.

6. This does not happen once but happens always. It is not time-based but is the eternal nature of things. This Someone comes from my being and is taken into my being, for the intimacy is complete. This intimacy provides a bliss of exquisite quality compared to which every other, even the most absorbing, is like water.

7. Whereas the resonance, the supreme Word is identified with myself, so that I am the Word; the Energy is felt as one with me but not precisely me. I possess the Energy, I am energetic, but am not the Energy. Without her I feel inertia, I am lifeless and can do nothing valid. With her my acts are real and authentic, and I am present in my acts, fully conscious.

8. Although I desire to find my counterpart, she will come only if I fall into the deep sleep, abandoning all thought, all desire and all action; going deep into sacrifice, waiting in the tomb, impassive, expectant, obedient. Then, beyond all imagining she comes, unexpectedly.

9. She is given to me. Now there is Someone to whom I can give myself entirely, for whom I can sacrifice myself, for whom I can become nothing; someone who cannot exist without me and without whom I cannot exist; someone who comes into being because of me and yet, paradoxically, is given to me.

10. I am the Image of the One who cannot be named. I imagine the One who proceeds from me and comes to me, who is like me and yet so different from me. This imagining is a realization, not a fiction. It is the ultimate exercise of authority. The imagining is not just from the mind or heart, just visual or auditory but physical too, sensation projecting sensation and body imagining body. The Counterpart wants to be imagined. That which is not influences that which is; the void affects the full.

11. The Spirit both proceeds from me and is given to me. I both master the Spirit and surrender to the Spirit. This fine balance is exciting, occurring at the very point of infinity. She is the fine point, the ultimate limit, the most sensitive and hidden, the inner sanctum. With her power I touch her, the Power. I know the sacred.

12. This touch involves all faculties and energies, the whole person. Mastering comes first, then surrender; but the mastering is useless unless it gives way to surrender. The two continue, neither eliminating the other, for the Spirit proceeds from the Father and Son.

13. Energy is at play. The greatest act of energy is to breath forth God and to surrender to the God of my making, the Spirit proceeding from me and given to me. And so, I come to know the One who is.

14. I have the authority, the power, the will and the pleasure to do this. It is done in utter restfulness and activity. As I sit here in perfect rest the Spirit springs from me. Restful activity! Knowledge and confidence and conviction are the basis from which the Energy arises, like water from the rock.

15. The *śakti*, which pours out of me in the stillness of meditation, coagulates and takes on the form of the woman and with her I am joined. This in turn empowers me in my stillness. Stillness and energy coincide in vibration and the whole panoply of creation springs as the expression of our union.

16. Your presence arouses in me that power that had lain dormant, unknown. It was for the sake of you that I did all these things. You inspired me to do "things improbable and impossible", to go to the depths and to remake the heavens and the earth.

17. All things lay possible in you. All worlds lay hidden in you. The possibility, which is revealed in you, is perfectly suited to the capacity in me. You arouse in me the energy that flows in me and circulates in the space of your being. So, I become alive.

18. I want you to be; and you inspire me to want you to be. You are given to me, complex Person! You are the junction holding all in unity. I rejoice in you and will not cease to delight in your incomprehensibility, for you are within my grasp and yet elude my grasp, enticing, puzzling, wonderful.

19. My thoughts turn not only to you the beautiful, whose eyes so captivate me, not only to you, Mary of Nazareth, from whom all femininity takes it name; but rather to all in ages past and ages future who spring from you, Spirit of God.

20. The poor who cry and those who look for someone to look on them: to them my heart goes out. These I can validly claim and address since I have lain in the tomb. And when I turn to them you turn to me, O Spirit, you who come to me in them.

21. Infinite love seeks the infinitely lovable and the impossible to love, for love conquers all and makes the unlovable lovable.

22. I will love this Project, for she is of me, mine. I hold the Project close since she is my very self. What will happen from our union?

23. In the complete satisfaction of our union, there is the entry into a new domain, and the acknowledgment of utter mystery: not the Void before union but the Void after union, the One completely Ineffable.

24. Although I am equally confident that the Spirit will come to me, I do not as yet know when or what delight will come or how the Spirit will come, or what will happen, or what will be revealed. I do not know.

25. By projecting the Spirit, I become spirit. By union with the Father I acquire the authority to project Spirit. I am what I do.

III.4

Conspiracy

sāhitya

1. I have surrendered and go into the deep sleep, which is the perfection of hope. From my body, from my very self you draw her out, she who rests there hidden. From the deepest level, the deepest sleep, you draw her out and bring her to me. And I see her who is taken from me and given to me, not in time but eternally.

2. The Spirit is there, before me, surprising, beautiful, unexpected yet suitable. She is not some figment of the imagination but real and active. She is the Window of opportunity, the Spirit of the Word.

3. You looked upon the Word you had spoken, Father, and you were pleased. The Spirit is your assent to me. She is your mark of approval, your sign of favour. She is not some emotion on your part, not an idea or an attitude, but a Person. Her coming is the incontrovertible evidence that you love me.

4. Yours is not some empty-handed approval but reward, empowerment and possession. You have given me someone to love and claim as my own. She is Proof of your approval. My soul's Delight is the evidence of your delight in me. She is the living expression, the personal expression, the hypostasis of your delight. I take pleasure in the pleasure you take in me.

5. I love her since she is the outcome of your love for me. I love her since she is from me and for me. I love her because she comes of her own free will. I love her because of herself, for she is inherently lovely.

6. Therefore, we work together. You work first; I work in cooperation with you. We project together, not an object but a Person. There is nothing more paradoxical than to project a centre of freedom, the Third Person.

7. This is my justice: that what I want to receive is what you, Father, want to give. We have the same will; we coincide.

8. How does she address him whom she does not call Father? But she, then, does not address him since she is not Word.

9. Only if I acknowledge the primacy and superiority of the One can I receive the Spirit as a gift. Only if I acknowledge the power of my own self can I project the Spirit. If I refuse the primacy of the One, there can be no gift. If I deny the power of my own self, there can be no projection. The Spirit is at once gift and project, received and emitted, of my self and not of my self. The Spirit is a conspiracy. Without the dual origin there is either arrogance or servility, overestimation or underestimation, sheer folly in any case.

10. If there were no Third Person how could I express the authority that arises in me? I would be forever a child in your eyes, not Son. I would be idle, not Lord.

11. The First Person crowns the Second Person with you, the Third. You are my glory, my honour, my prize, not made of laurel but the Third, the Final Person. Forever I will say: "This at last is my counterpart, taken from me, given to me", and I will unite with you, not for the thousand years but in an eternal interchange. So, you are my Delight, O Spirit, and I taste you and relish the taste.

12. I now invite you to myself, and dedicate myself to you, and invite you to inhabit me in body, mind and spirit; in harmony with the One who is, for are you not his gift to me, coming also as your own gift to me! Spirit understood and inspiring, indwelling in a way I did not understand.

13. The relationship of Giver, Receiver and Given: this is the divine Reality, the ultimate Communion.

14. All these thoughts bring the deepest level to light. Once it is known I return and rest in a silence beyond words, in the velvet night of love.

III.5

Goddess

devī

1. Father, you freely give her, she who is freedom, she who is freely received. She freely accepts to be given to the one whom she freely chooses for herself and her self-giving makes him freely choose her. Thus, freedom rings through all its changes.

2. Elusive Spirit, ever transcendent, ever beyond, ever to be attained, enticing and attractive, whom I know and seek to know! How could I seek to know you if I did not already perceive unconsciously all that you are. There is no trace of anxiety but great confidence, assurance and stability so that the *śakti* dances upon the platform of flesh.

3. There is the sense of the Third, the one who proceeds from me and is given to me, the sense of the One who spins herself out of nothing, the self-emanated who dispels all our ideas and theories, the completely surprising. For if the Spirit is God, truly, then she is her own source, not apart from the other Two but neither just their instrument. This is exhilarating.

4. This is where I really live, where I really find myself and am fulfilled: this union with Kālī / Spirit. Here is the fullness of maturity.

5. The sense of authority arises, the sense of power and vitality, because you are there, mysterious, present, open, receptive, enticing. Already because of the union I have with the One, there is a sense of authority. He is the basis, you are the opportunity. He is a source of the spring; you are the space into which all flows.

6. You are given by the Father, you are projected by the Son, yes, but you also arise of your own volition. Otherwise you would not be the Third divine Person, consubstantial with the Father and the Son. You are free.

7. You have selected me. Around my neck you have placed the garland of your choice. You have made me your champion, and your choice awakens me. The kiss of your lips raises me from death. Once reduced to silence, your touch now gives me voice and I exclaim.

8. You are intimate to me and no one will ever know you as I have known you. We are secret to each other, out in the desert together among the palms. We have closed the windows of the world, and here in this quiet place, in this darkness, we dwell together, incomparable, hidden and revealed, subject to subject yet one subject, one body.

9. Now the time has come. You are the Divine Spirit, always given, always to be attained, always known and always to be discovered, infinite and inexhaustible. You are forever secret and forever revealed, with secret opening onto secret, as I explore the corridors of your being. You are the gift that is forever being given, never taken for granted, always to be received, gift containing gift within gift, suited to me.

10. Out of myself I project you, and by this same energy I spin you and take delight in you, turning you in every direction and enjoying you from every angle. Then suddenly I notice that this is why you wanted me. This is what you wanted from the start. Before ever I began to project, you were there, hidden, as yet unrealised. Though concealed you existed. Though not directing things, you decided their course, O Extraordinary One.

11. And you choose me and take pleasure in me because I have acted freely and have freely done what you wanted. You are the acknowledgment of the knowledge. Your coming is the approval of my being and the justification of my behaviour. I am filled with comfort at your approval.

12. You satisfy me for you are completely God and for God, showing in your eyes the intelligence of God, and in your demeanour the mercy of God. You have the energy of God and invite into God. The grace of your appearance is both divine and human, reflecting all divinity and all possibility, suited to the One from whom all comes. This is what completely enthrals me. Our relationship is of depth to depth, God to God, the most profound of secrets.

III.6

Person

puruṣa

1. Individuality is not the same as personhood. When I abandon the limited concept of the person as individual then I perceive the Spirit as person.

2. When I have become the Word, I perceive the Spirit. Only when I abandon the sense of the ego and the attitude of 'me' or 'mine', and take on the new self, perceiving myself as the Self, only then do I perceive the Spirit. Only when I have become the Second Person can I perceive the Third.

3. When I bring all things into harmony with the Word, then a sweetness appears, an approval deeper than a good conscience, a softness supremely subtle, coming from outside and entering right into the self, an intimacy quite different from the indwelling presence of the First Person.

4. It is not something I seek to achieve. It is! And I acknowledge it. It is given, and I assent to it. It is not something, which is absent and which I must produce but something present, which I acknowledge.

5. I sit in complete stillness, gathering the whole world around me in affirmation and blessing; but that is not enough. Gradually, wonderfully, the Spirit appears at the centre so that all become the jewels of her adornment. Here at last is a centre to the universe, a heart where I can place my heart. Here at last is someone whom I can love, freely, forever, with no let of ecstasy, no break in communion. Here is someone for whom I can be love and the messenger of love.

6. Here, indeed, is someone whom I can love and rouse to love, and whose rousing arouses me in love, who is consumed and absorbed in love by my loving and takes me into love even as she is consumed. Her cry of delight enwraps me and takes me beyond, into your love, O One Who Is! Who is the lover, the loved and the love?

7. From the outset, when first the music sounded and drew me into the desert, you were leading me to yourself, O One Who Is! And you wanted me to be the Word from whom all things come so that you could love me. And you wanted me to be the messenger of love to the listening Sprit.

8. Why so long in coming into the desert of my soul, O Spirit? No matter the length of the journey, the prize is magnificent!

9. The Spirit is God, and therefore almighty. The First and Second Persons are powerless until the Spirit chooses. Yet the Spirit chooses what is best and most suited to herself. The Power chooses the Powerful.

10. The Spirit is not just the bond of love between Father and Son. This depersonalises the Spirit who ceases to be God. The Spirit too is free, has initiative and choice, has the same majesty and Godhead as Father and Son. There is an ultimacy about the Spirit.

11. You love me, Spirit, because I am the perfect expression of the Ineffable. I am totally and essentially one with Him and delight to be his perfect image. I delight to have his authority and to hold all things in unity in my self. And yet, it is only you, in your freedom, who chooses to choose and to come to me. And your coming brings me to being, so that I am most truly myself and become most truly the image of the Ineffable. It is so that you might choose me that I first heard the music calling me into the desert.

III.7

Break

viccheda

1. You are splendid in your fury. Who can resist you? Your look, which welcomes and incites, turns to scorn when your displeasure is aroused. Your look can warm or chill. Your smile brings to knowledge; your frown consigns to darkness. Without raising a finger, you make or break. You judge with your whole person. Who can resist such power?

2. Your refusal is terrible, for what is the purpose of our being except yourself. We cannot choose you if you do not choose us. What weapons can we take up when our energy is removed, and our purpose gone?

3. But I do not fear you since love cannot resist love; you cannot refuse those who wait in hope. I look at you without hesitation; you will not refuse me since we are destined for each other. I am confident since all proceeds from me. I am the Word, and the energy that springs from me is your own self.

4. But I delight in your fire, which lifts up and throws down. Here is the intensity of truth. Your smile has meaning since your frown is terrible. Your judgment is incisive. Therefore, I respect you and your look justifies me.

5. Before you I become real in a way I was not before. My whole being, my whole body, every fibre is charged and quivers. I tremble as the once solid body is made liquid and subtle, and I am drawn out and move towards you. It is the surrender to your attraction. See how you unmake me!

6. Again, the closer I come to you the less I can speak. The more I become the Word to you, the less I can have recourse to words. The Word is made perfect in Silence. So, I describe the descent into silence, which is not absence of Word but its perfection. Again, see how you make me by unmaking me.

7. To you I give no name. No words describe you; no category holds you. The mind collapses in your presence. 'Thou!' In this address is the divine intercourse, which overflows into bodily sensations. This is the intercourse, which all bodily intercourse seeks to achieve. 'I and Thou'? We go beyond 'I' and 'Thou'. See how you unmake us both!

8. It is one thing to bring all into harmony, all the contrary elements, to bring them into harmony within my body, my being, and to become all these things. It is another to surrender to the unexpected presence who comes and takes me into a joy I could not imagine.

9. All authority is given to me. Authority is first experienced as the ability to do, to express, to govern, and to produce. But it is complete only when it becomes its opposite: the surrender to beauty and to person and to grace.

10. A quietness descends and a stillness upon me;
    a permission is given, an allowing;
    and suddenly, Kālī, you arise in fury,
    in splendour your fire breaks out, consuming, warming.
    And I am taken up in the exultation of your power.

III.8

Mystery

rahasya

1. You are elusive. You are possibility, opportunity, the expectant silence, the unknown, waiting to be explored. You are the dream, the beauty within beauty, the suggestion, so fleeting and so attractive, drawing us ever upwards.

2. You have come to me. I take you and possess you, my Spirit. Freely I take you; it is right that I take, for you are given to me, and freely I claim my inheritance. Obediently, too, I take you since I am from Him whose Word I am. In every way, with my whole being, I take you and enter into your mystery.

3. And this excites me, for it means entering into the unknown, away from all I have been, from all my securities. Voices of fear cry out, "Do not go!" Yet for this was I pronounced. To the Spirit whose mystery I enter I say: "Come with me into the path of your person which I will explore, and you too shall know." For the mystery is hidden from the mystery. Down the path, as in the cave of jewels, there are joys guessed and unimagined, both known and unknown. Where will this lead us? To good or ill? Not to good in the way we have known good before. Forbidden, yes, but only by false gods. And so, I enter you, Spirit mine, and I forget all I ever was.

4. Falling, falling into you, the great abyss, rising, rising to heights I never knew, not to the level of everyday consciousness but to the heart, to the light that is brilliant with darkness, the darkness that is brilliant with light.

5. You are received. You are given only to those who have lived by the Word and become the Word. Deep within you have inspired us. In your absence you have been the target, the distant goal, the outline hardly seen, calling with unutterable softness across the wide plains, evanescent and all the more enticing, beautiful with entrancing beauty.

6. In order to attain that beauty, I have lived my life and spoken my words and seen the outpouring of my blood. But now you are given to me. You come into my tomb and surprise me.

III.9

Beauty

prabhāsa

1. I had left the city and gone into the desert, to the One Who Is. The resonance of the Word has played in me and I now perceive the freedom of the Spirit.

2. The whole world disappears when you stand before me, your eyes like deep pools. All else is opaque, without lustre, as though blind, but your eyes are inviting, opening onto endless possibility. They puzzle me and ask me the question, 'What shall you do? Who shall you be?'

3. Yes, I will go down this path, plunging into the dark corridors of your dwelling, rejecting all else as chattel. Body, mind, heart, spirit: the whole person plunges into your womb. Entering into a depth the opens onto further depths, in an infinite trajectory, an endless experience of delight.

III.10

Coming

abhyāgama

1. Let me take you into my heart, you who come from me. For I am lonely. I am not alone if the Father is with me, yet I am desolate until you come. I will enfold you and cover you and you will dwell there like a bird in its bower.

2. I know you are present, that you come from me and are given to me. But until you manifest yourself inside of me and outside of me, I remain closed and cold. Come, Spirit, and release me.

3. You come to me, and I become myself. You awaken in me knowledge that lay dormant, knowledge I knew but did not realise. I am, yet I become what I am because you are there. I am the Word but now I can speak. Your presence arouses me. All my faculties come alive, vibrant, rushing like sparks through the tinder. At last you have come to me, long awaited. We meet out of time and place, where nothing inhibits us, nothing disturbs us. You come and so I come.

4. You surprise me, always new, always unexpected, revealing depth within depth. You come to my heart and nestle there in your rightful chamber. Disturb me, entrance me, you who are so like me and so unlike me, heart of my heart, mind of my mind, "flesh of my flesh" (Genesis 2:23). For I recognise you: you are myself, so other than myself, my other self and I so take you.

5. I love you, Spirit. Come to me! I have sacrificed my life to find you. Come and make me happy with a happiness that transports me into the unknown, there to know the Unknowable, from whom you come. Let me touch you so that together we can fly through the air in the heights.

6. Come, Holy Spirit, descend upon me bodily, upon my body, heart upon my heart to make it leap; enwrap my mind with your mind so that it may expand. Come, grace upon my grace, gift upon gift. Come Spirit upon my spirit, depth calling to depth and we shall meet as one in the One. Empower my power, for without you I am powerless, a mere corpse, a lifeless thing, enmeshed in the absurd and the repetitious.

7. Come with me into the silence. Come into the desert and listen to the wind. Come into the mysterious dark and see the Unseen. I have been this way before and it is wonderful.

8. It is because I communicate the Person of the Father that the Spirit is drawn to me. Although she is herself the Gift of the Father, she is also drawn to me whose very essence is the Word, the Word of Love, of the Father. That is the wonder of my being. She wants to contemplate in me the One from whom she comes and whom she knows in me.

9. I rejoice to be the expression of the Inexpressible and the manifestation of the Unmanifestable, to be the revelation of the Hidden. I am the acclamation "I am" of the One who is most truly 'I am'.

10. This appeals to the Spirit who draws near to me in this knowledge and wishes to contemplate in me the One from whom she comes. She knows the Giver through the One who expresses him.

III.11

Freedom

svātantrya

1. You have shown your freedom, which nothing must constrain. So, I wait for your command, but your command is subtle. You command me to be commanding. You do this because you see my freedom. You invite me to be assertive. You permit me to take control. Your freedom requires my freedom, you wish me to be free with you: two freedoms, one freedom.

2. I must wait. For what? That is uncertain. The *śakti* comes in her own way at her own time. Desire must be purified till it becomes pure obedience, pure readiness, always willing, always true servant of the *śakti*. Then she comes as a grace. With all one's strength and capacity and talents and power, one is simply the servant of the *śakti*. She may come; she may not. This waiting is difficult to endure. It is very subtle. I wait for her but she enables me to await. She makes me want to take her. She freely makes me free with her. When I surrender to her she surrenders to me. So, I am justified and authorised. She is the proof that I am true. Her coming gives me power.

3. All is from me; all is for me, the Name who names. But this cannot satisfy or puzzle me. You come suddenly. But where do you come from? You appear as flesh from my flesh, freedom from my freedom, freedom taking me captive. I find myself free in you, with a freedom I did not know, for to be free with the free is freedom indeed. I am free in the vast space of the Unrestrained, the Unpredictable, the Evernew.

4. You come, and I am amazed. Where do you come from? How are you possible? Here at last is someone to whom I can surrender. I surrender my authority to you. Why? Authority becomes full when it is given away. It is received in freedom and surrendered in freedom.

5. And so, I see you, the Person from the Persons, the Person of the Persons, the Third Person, the most truly Personal, for your Person reveals our Persons. In you at last we are fully personal.

6. O Kālī / Spirit, you freely want to be the result of my freedom. You freely choose to be subject to me and to be empowered by me who am empowered by you. How to understand these paradoxes? There is no understanding since we move into the mystery, the experience that transcends all our mental constructions. There is deeper enjoyment here.

III.12

Satiation

tarpaṇa

1. My opportunities, my time and talents have been used up in the confused search for you. All has been an offering to you, seeking to take my rest in you, O fearsome Divinity. What a journey it has been! My life has been a sacrifice in your honour. Will you give yourself to me and give me the joy in body and soul and spirit that I seek and that you have made me seek? You have touched me with your veil so as to make me turn to you!

2. So, I waited, and my waiting was worship, for by it I acknowledge you as supreme, O Third Person, Ultimate Person, Person of the Persons.

3. Not for the Father primarily, nor for the Son, but only for you, O Spirit. You have the primacy of the Third.

4. There is something worth surrendering; there is someone worth surrendering to. I surrender my authority to you, Spirit! Why? Because it is right. All authority comes to its highest state when it is given as gift. It is surrendered in freedom and received in freedom.

5. Paradoxically, light is the manifestation of wonderful darkness. Fullness is the expression of the Void, coming from the Void, based on the Void and revealing the Void. The more we are aware of the Void the more we feel power moving in us, which is due to the Void that transcends it.

6. There is the other Void, the Space into which all my wealth is poured. There is the welcome, the smile of pleasure, the acceptance and favour. She is given, as an opportunity and grace, not to make up for an inadequacy but to provide relevance for the capacity. The Space reflects the Void, the open heart, the care. I move into mystery that was otherwise unavailable. Together we reach the heights, as I move into her.

III.13

Smile

hāsa

1. I take you to myself because you are beautiful. How shall I not take you since you are necessary? I cannot be without you. So, I take you and hold you. I choose and hold, total in my choice, unflagging, calm. All else disappears and you alone are captivating.

2. What else could I want since it is you I seek in every wish? Searching for you I had walked other paths but now that I have found you, my footsteps cease. Around you I swirl, above and below, on every side, you, the centre of my being.

3. I choose you. No one else can claim this pleasant realm where I place my affection, the one whom I embrace.

4. You are gentle yet bewildering, approachable yet requiring all: pure and purifying. You are timeless, shimmering with light, rich with hidden treasures, a world to explore and know.

5. Do you like me? Do you want me? Am I necessary to you? The answer must be yes or I am lost. But how shall I know? If I do not know how will I be justified? If I am not justified, how shall I live? I will be only a worthless thing, rejected, guilty, condemned.

6. You incite me to love. You are entirely yourself, without ambiguity or irresolution. Your purity and truth, your totality and openness, the possibility of going into your soul, your delightful inmost being—these arouse the love in me that lay dormant. And so, I join myself to you and you to me.

7. And I enjoy the coming of the Spirit with the roar of a mighty wind and the tumult of the waves, as I sit here still in meditation.

8. As I sit here with the sense of Śivahood and its emanative power, there comes a sense of approval, a sense of affirmation that comes from the most mysterious of sources. It is the *śakti* making her choice and revealing herself to me. It is the Dove descending bodily and communicating the wordless word of love. It is so soft, so delicate, it can be heard only in utter stillness and purity.

9. It is in the calm of my conscience that I know you have received me, in the peace, in the totality of my involvement. I can place myself in you because you receive me without vacillation. You are the target of my arrow, clear and pristine. I hold you fast and pierce you with the fine point of the soul.

10. I find satisfaction and I know you approve, for you say "yes" with all your person. You approve my intent; our wills are one. Word and Spirit unite in their interplay, for who gives, who receives? Both give and are given, both receive and are received.

11. You teach me, not by words but by your smile or your frown. You demand the best of me so that I become the Word that alone satisfies you. You teach but not as the Word teaches. You draw me out, as at the beginning you drew creation out. By your teaching stone turns to wheat, the fish spread wings and the smile appears on earth.

12. At the thought of the consort whom I would project and who would be mine, who would be given to me and who would come to me, a smile crept over my face, the smile of lasting joy.

13. There is projection so that there might be encounter; and in the encounter to go into the depths. This occurs in ever increasing cycles, again and again: the vibration is infinite.

III.14

Groan

HĀ-HĀ

1. You are beautiful in your vulnerability. Here I can do something and perform a worthwhile act. Here is someone I can serve totally, bringing happiness and knowledge.

2. The idea of Kālī appeals to me. More than the idea: the reality of the goddess profoundly satisfies me. More even, her fulfilment: the Holy Spirit. The realization, not only that she chooses me but also that she is given to me and that I am given to her, produces a profound groan of pleasure, a real groan from the depths, for I have arrived at truth given by the One beyond all knowledge.

III.15

Descent of the Spirit

śaktipāta

1. There was no one to lead me, no guru, no teacher. The ones who did present themselves as teachers did me harm, not perceiving the grace that was at work in me. It was by your light alone that I have found a way through the thickets and that I now stand on the open plain, the vista stretching before me. Only you could guide me. I refused all the others, eventually so that you, Spirit, would teach me to be myself and to seek you and to form you and to love you and together with you enter into the Silence.

2. Although we may yearn for the 'gross' and the senses, it is really at the supreme level that we find rest and satisfaction. Here we commune best. With you, O Spirit, we can dare to do the impossible: to be God and project God, and to unite with God and to go beyond God.

3. You have taught me, Spirit, not by words but by your guiding touch when you descended upon me. You took me through ways and experiences, sights and relationships, till the image of the Word was found in me; so that I could know my self and the Self, my truth and the Truth and so find the Christ of the Gospel. I have found my Christ and can say yes to him and to myself, for I have found the one in whom I can have faith and by whom I can have faith in myself.

4. It has been an immensely long journey, lonely and distressed. You alone could teach me, Hidden Power, and you have brought me to my power. You have made me come alive, Kālī of the Spirit. You have aroused me and I am. You yourself have initiated me and I have become my Self and see that I am Bhairava.

5. What I wish to do now I have in fact done from the start, little did I know it! I have indeed been initiated by the Spirit herself and brought to love.

6. You assent to be the Spirit who derives from me. You awaken in me powers that could only appear in relationship with you. You make me be for you. Indeed, you make me be, since to be without you is effectively not to be.

7. When I ask the question of you, Kālī, "Do you love me, do you want me?" there is like a cloud, a soft cloud that descends upon me, a realm of possibility and opportunity. The breath becomes slower and deeper, the profoundest sigh, relaxing, a realization that a world enticing and wonderful is laid before me, and an excitement rises from the base of my being and I enjoy you. This is the tantra.

III.16

Pleasure

kāma

1. Spirit, as you descend you enliven my spirit. The sweetest pleasure fills my spirit, such as no wine of the grape can give. You enliven my mind with perceptions I never had before, the finest truth. You lead me on a merry dance into unknown realms. I know you in the depth and at the uttermost distance. My arrow flies to you in one great arc and attains you, delicately, firmly, in a touch that sparkles. And I succumb to your thrall.

2. You give my life a life it never knew. You heighten every faculty and sense and bring my body to its finest orgasm, the orgasm that comes from above, not from the mind or the will. It is the orgasm that comes from the wisdom of the Spirit. For you must touch the body and fulfil its every wish. You cannot be absent from the flesh. The whole range of enjoyment fills me, every *chakra* spins. You evolve my body to its fullest capacity; body becomes spirit and yet remains body.

3. The lethargy and heaviness, the opaqueness and transience of matter are gone, transformed from within. You excite every dimension, awakening every memory, every hope. The lights are exquisite such as no paint or glass can produce. The touch is satisfied. The imagination is aroused and fulfilled.

4. In the calm and the stillness, I enjoy the pleasuring of your love. Without anxiety or haste I enjoy you and all your gifts. I breathe deeply into myself the pleasure you give. This is my joy, my reality, my purpose.

5. You make love from within, not just in the mind or in the heart, but in the limbs as well, an abiding love that does not draw away. It is the foretaste of the resurrection.

6. You come upon me bodily, O Spirit, and transform my body, elevating me through each centre till I am whole and utterly transfigured by your coming. I am indeed a *tāntrika*.

III.17

Fluid

sara

1. Distinctions melt and we become liquid, flowing one into the other. This all too solid flesh softens. From you, from your inmost being, from your bliss and your anticipation of bliss, flows the ambrosia. The stream issuing from you excites me so that I flow towards you. The two currents swirl and mingle in ever new combinations, giving and receiving, exciting and producing, causing more and more to flow, as we move from solid to subtle to supreme.

2. I can rest in your heart, O Spirit, only when I become spirit. I can feel you drawing the finest essences from my body, and I surrender. Take! The transient flesh is transformed into spirit, producing the fine point of emotion, that perfect drop, that distillation that is placed—O with what delight—in your heart. O Spirit, you demand, not that I cease to be flesh, but that my flesh become spirit.

3. Thus, I am for you, you for me. I am present to you and you to me, gift to gift, choice of choice. I acknowledge that you are of me and I of you, differently yet one. Your spirit calls on me and unlocks a reservoir I did not know. We are complementary.

4. The pleasure of our union courses through my veins, healing and invigorating, soothing and stimulating. We remain still and observe and enjoy. We are so still, even as the great stream surges, in me, in you, from me to you, from you to me, in one body. There is enjoyment, there is devouring. The heavens open and I know the One Who Is.

III.18

Destruction

dhvaṃsa

1. You will not come to me unless first I shed my blood; for you seek the finest essence. You will smile on me when I have known the height and the depth, vulnerability and drunkenness of soul, for you demand the best. You will bring me to yourself and give me your power when I first die. You are splendid and troubling, desirable yet destroying.

2. Spirit, for your sake and to win you, I submitted to pouring out my life in sacrifice. The frightful desolation—so total and so long—was a saving act, for then the consoling Spirit, perceived and appreciated without limit, came upon me and upon all.

III.19

Awareness

saṁvit

1. Your presence brings me to awareness. Increasingly, from the root of my being, each faculty begins to flower, from the lowest to the highest. It is the rising of the coiled and dormant power, which begins to function, taking me to the highest heaven. It is the flow of the Spirit, like the river Jordan that traverses the arid land and brings it to flower. Each faculty awakens in due order, more and more subtly, with increasing illumination until at last I realize with full consciousness that 'I am' in every way. Only you can show me this truly.

III.20

Restraint

nirodha

1. The intimation of your presence makes me still, both introvert and extrovert, both outgoing and recollected; restraining both the outward and the inward. And I sense arising in me delight and freedom, expansiveness and satisfaction.

2. At dawn, between night and day, between sleep and activity I sit balanced, and sense the vitality rising. It is the middle path, the most delicate of channels, the inmost vein of the lotus stalk. I am fully attentive and universal, rejoicing in the energy that has become manifest. The breath slows down, becoming clear and easy, heralding the Spirit.

3. I welcome you, and by the power you awaken in me, take hold of you and arouse you. You empower and sanctify all the centres of my being. We cooperate.

4. Then comes a sense of union with you, as Śiva with *śakti*, not rapid and unsavoured but with full intention and attention, restrained, going deeper and deeper into the act.

5. The resultant bliss heals and sanctifies increasingly.

III.21

Play

krīḍa

1. You lead me on, playfully, taking me away from all thoughts and plans. You lead me into your passion and your fire. What freedom and lack of constraint! You seek the best, drawing me out of myself and casting away the chaff. You are in control and without control, a driving wind blowing as you will.

2. O destructive Enchantress, you unleash power in me, energy arousing energy! I am wild with passion, sitting here still in meditation.

3. I say "Yes!" to the dance. You have sprung from me and I spring after you, and we fly like insects in the summer air. You have come to me and overwhelmed me with your freedom. I am freed and purified by your flood.

4. The free movement of energy swirls around the body, in the emotions and in the mind, in the whole person. This is noted and received, without any attempt to understand or control. It is enjoyed.

5. Where will you take me, as we run through the woods away from the town? But now I enter calmly into your space. The frenzy of change is over and all I know is the radiance of your fire. To you, quite simply, I am.

III.22

Intercourse

maithuna

1. The Spirit is received by the Son as a gift from the Father. The Son does not give the Spirit to the Father. Thus, although the Spirit proceeds from both Father and Son, the Spirit proceeds from them differently: from the Father as Giver and from the Son as Receiver, for reception is also a determinant and an act.

   The Spirit proceeds freely from the Son, as a wave, a surging within the Son and from the Son. The Spirit also penetrates into the Son by his reception of the gift.

   Thirdly, because the Spirit is God the Spirit arises spontaneously from the Spirit herself. She appears freely, uncaused, both proceeding from Father and Son and arising spontaneously of her own accord. This last is most mysterious, and she comes to the Son as her own self-giving to him.

   The interplay of Spirit proceeding from the Son and giving herself freely to the Son is experienced in the human body. Indeed, it is the paradigm of sexual intercourse, its origin and criterion. The more intensely and extensively it is experienced in prayer, the less need there is for physical intercourse.

2. I do not want that surge of orgasm even though, extraordinary and delightful, it reveals heaven itself. I do not want it since it passes. There must be another way, calmer and more enduring, engaging mind and will as much as emotions and body. To be a *tāntrika*, in the thousand year, indeed the eternal embrace of she who is a counterpart—this is the solution. This is the embrace at

the origin of all embracing in love. It is felt in every faculty and situation. Essentially, in every substance, there is intercourse. This I recognise in the calm of knowledge; and from that knowledge flows the emotion that satisfies the heart. I now know abidingly that which orgasm allows me to glimpse for a moment.

3. I wish to be roused by your presence. I wish to be excited by the possibility of our intercourse, to touch your freshness and grace, and to dwell there, ever about to act, ever about to emit but arresting the flow and so entering new realms.

    I wish neither to suppress the eagerness, nor to satisfy the desire. Rather, I wish with all my heart to hold the excitement at its climax because from the outset I have known that this is the way to enter through the narrow door.

    Our union is complete and on-going; our bodies, our lives and emotions flow together as one, mutually related, fully expanded.

    At this point we stand at the origin and end of the world. All is seen to come from our union and to be consummated in our intercourse. The heavens open and remain open. All times and seasons are found in us, every purpose of mind and hand is fulfilled in our mutuality. Every authority is ours, and every pleasure.

4. There is the capacity, the urge, the massed willingness to perform the act of intercourse but not the act itself. It is the double contrasting movement, the drive to intercourse and the restraint from intercourse, the one moment, the balancing on the knife edge, supremely difficult.

    As a result, there is the build up of sexual energy but not the loss of semen. This excitement opens up the heavens. It is the intimate relationship, perceived throughout the ages, between human sexuality and divine consciousness.

5. As I attend to you and receive you, doors open, in a long corridor. I penetrate more fully into you, discovering you and becoming myself. The coverings fall away and you are revealed, and I become what I have always been. Ultimately, we are simply Śiva and śakti, you my counterpart, my freedom, my light, my joy. You are revealed as the Spirit to my Word.

6. From our union there springs a double movement: the ascension into Love, and the benediction of the earth, like the sun emitting its rays. It is a new fruitfulness outside the cycle of birth and death.

7. What will I not do for you? I will give you stars for jewels, and fetch pearls from the sea. But what can I really offer you? Blood and seed? Yes! And also what they represent. I take you to myself and offer you myself. I take you and enjoy you. I have the authority to take you and to enjoy you who come from me and come of yourself and are given to me from above, with the divine command to take and make one body. I offer myself to you and join myself to you. So, I give my all and receive all.

8. This interplay opens up ever wider dimensions till its communion is as wide as the universe, giving and receiving every value till indeed heaven is given to heaven and love loves love.

9. I have conquered you. You are mine. In all gentleness I have overcome all your resistance, all your ruses, and shown myself to be the stronger. So, I take you and hold you, the prize of my victory, and plunge deep into you, and glory in your submission.

10. Or is this your highest ruse, that you have trapped me in our embrace? So be it! I surrender to my conquest. We take each other and are taken. There is one taking.

III.23

Degrees

prakrama

1. Sight is wonderful, touch is beautiful, but they pass. The encounter is exhilarating, its memory is wonderful, but I want it to last. The union of a thousand nights is haunted by the shadow of its end and is 'gross' *(sthūla)*. I want a lasting union. There must, therefore, be a new way to touch, a new way to see, which surpasses the passing moment and contains it.

   Let us go back to the origin, or go far into the future. Let us expand and intensify. Let us know both the joys of life and their passing value, and then let us seek the heightened pleasure that does not pass.

   Let us not be held by time but go beyond it, confidently reaching into the unknown, beyond even the subtle *(sūkṣma)* that lasts longer, to a new plane, to the supreme *(para)* state of union which lasts for ever, to the highest level where reality itself is known as the intercourse of Word and Spirit.

   The highest level does not suppress the lower. The lower continues, indeed it helps sustain the higher.

2. I know what sex means, and assent to its possibility, yet withhold from the act. I can imagine the act but do not fantasize or seek gratification from the fantasy. This knowledge helps establish my self-image and my character. It provides the analogue.

3. The subtle level is an assent to the body and to the states and functioning of the body. It involves a knowledge of the external, the 'gross' *(sthūla)* level, a rejoicing and assent. They are useful to each other and confirm each other.

4. If the ecstasy depends on physical contact, it must indeed pass, for touch is passing. But if it is based on the Eternal Feminine, the supreme Spirit, it lasts. It occurs forever, once and eternally. The Spirit touches every faculty and spiritualises every limb. In the intercourse of the Spirit flesh is transfigured in light.

III.24

Union

saṅghaṭṭa

1. I draw close to the one I admire; I want to be with him and concentrate on him and identify with him: a perfect union of hearts. Then a switch occurs and instead of facing him, I inhabit him and he inhabits me. We are two yet one, facing the same direction so to speak. We have merged.

2. So, I join forces with him. What shall we do to cement our identity? What act to perform that will truly unite us as one; what project, what work?

3. When I kiss her, he is kissing her; he knows my kiss of her and feels it as his own. Likewise I feel his kiss of her and feel it as my own. We share totally. Thus he and I both kiss her.

4. When I make love, it is the whole tribe of males also who make love. They feel the excitement and are not ignorant of the pleasure. In my name and in theirs I act. I see with my eyes, and I see with theirs. Their hands have formed my touch. I cannot act without them, for I do not exist without them, they have defined me. My body is theirs since we are committed to the same end. As I act, I act with their bodies as well, drawing strength from them, committing them. We are one body.

5. She too is identified with the whole tribe of women, so that in kissing her I feel the kiss of countless others who are present in her. Thus in her and my kiss countless men and women kiss each other. Each kiss is the universal kiss.

6. It goes further. In this universal kiss the divine kiss is known. The multiplicity of the kiss springs from the divine kiss; it is its expression.

7. Sometimes, there is the joining of sex to sex, but brought to a pitch of excitement without emission. There is no projection of semen, which would involve time and history and require a later generation to find the new path. Rather, in the stillness of the joining, at the same time as the union of sex to sex, mind is projected into mind, and heart is projected into heart. The outpouring of the heart is received into the cave of the heart, which first excited it and called for it.

8. Then the divine relationship is suddenly revealed and a gasp escapes from deep from within. There is, supremely, the union of destiny to destiny, grace to grace. The projection of one's very being has become heaven itself, the greatest projection, the supreme emission of 'seed', supremely exciting. All else fades by comparison.

9. Staying with the image and the appeal of the act but not proceeding to the performance produces a balance of inner and outer, exteriority and interiority. As a result, the energy moves into a different plane. A new possibility is opened up and the act is extended in meaning. An intercourse is achieved that is both more original and more future and more abiding – the intercourse of paradise, of the new heavens and the new earth.

III.25

Intimacy

sakhya

1. To me you give the entire world, *O Fons et Origo*, the whole panoply of the possible. All these are in me, from me, for me. But better than these is the Spirit whom you have given me to love, who comes from me and to whom I can surrender. I am with you, I am as your image, but the Other One proceeds both from you and from me, so that my relationship to her is different from my relationship to you. All is from you and, like myself, is with you, in union with you. But to her I can give all as an adornment and a garment. To her I can surrender, and in her I take my pleasure.

III.26

Mutual

anyonya

1. O Spirit, you fully express the Void as I do, but differently, for we are part and counterpart. I am Word fully revealing the Silence and you are Spirit fully revealing the Incomprehensible. We are for each other. It is the dialogue of Logos and non-Logos, of the one Paraclete and the other Paraclete, of non-Spirit and of Spirit. I precede you yet cannot be without you, for my whole being is directed to you, O Spirit rising like incense from my burning coal. I am made for you, to serve you, to be your support and your delight. In you I find rest and satisfaction. We are mutual.

2. You are the beauty I never knew, the wonder I never realised and I am rendered speechless before you. The Word falls silent before the Spirit, overwhelmed. But a renewed Word arises. The Word is now exclamation, when wonder has penetrated the Word.

3. The interplay is constant, each vibration opening up new vistas. The true Word becomes more truly Word, the Spirit more fully what she always was, in an expansion that has no limits, going from glory to glory, Light from Light, Light to Light, Light in Light, in the furnace of love.

4. The Word projects the Spirit; her presence makes the Word become itself. The Spirit empowers the Word, and in turn the Word makes the Spirit effective and fruitful. Her effectiveness means that the Word has been effective. This is the interaction of Word and Spirit. We are for each other, equal, reciprocal and not irrelevant.

5. Who proceeds from whom? For you arise in me but I achieve new heights through you.

III.27

Touch

sparśa

1. Immense confidence and quiet assuredness come together. Activity and restfulness coincide. There is no effort; all is natural, a simple flow. It is a holding and an imparting that is supra-sexual. The transmission is from the ever-increasing fountainhead of vitality.

2. This is due to the clear receptivity of the counterpart. The Spirit arouses the Word by perfect discipleship; the Word coming from transcendent Silence arises in the expectant Silence.

3. The Spirit inspires and touches. She comes to every faculty, every limb and aspect, even the most material, for the Spirit reaches from end to end. Sensitivity to the presence and transcendence of the Spirit, to her freedom and power, is the finest form of touch.

4. The meditator allows the touch to be felt in every way, sexually too since the human being is essentially sexual. The physical and emotional aspects of the touch are felt, the resurrecting of the body. But the sensitivity and surrender are possible only by being aware of one's own power and value. The complementarity of mutual power and surrender, taking and giving, oscillates with increasing intensity till it reaches the fine point, the infinite Void.

III.28

Fusion

sāmarasya

1. I wish to pour myself into you. I need to pour my heart and mind and body into you, and you into me, so that there is one mind, one heart, one body, flesh to flesh, touching, mingling in perfect fusion.

    But there is more. For I wish to mingle our lives and indeed our ultimate spirit, spirit to spirit.

    But there is more. By this great surge of power, which your every touch arouses in me. I want to seize all the worlds and give them to you.

    But there is more. Be the very Spirit of God to me so that I can be Word to you! Be eternal so that I can eternally be to you.

    And we are wrapt into the Stillness, all said, all done. Nothing more needs to be done since now there is All fused as One.

2. I am drawn close to you, companion of my days. We progress, part to counterpart, body to body, heart to heart, mind to mind, spirit to spirit, as the centres open and expand and lead one to the other. We penetrate ever deeper into each other and become ever more subtle and spiritual, so that flesh becomes spirit and time stands still in eternity.

3. To the Spirit I offer the body made spirit, the body transformed into spirit because of the attractive power of the Spirit. Spirit makes spirit. The spiritification of the body is not a dematerialisation but a transformation, a heightening of the body, an intensification. The potentiality of the body is now fully actual.

III.29

Enclosing

saṃpuṭa

1. To whom is the Word eternally addressed if not to the Spirit? Who shall hear eternally if not the Spirit given to the Word? Sound and silence, silence and sound. How shall the sound be heard if not in silence; silence evokes the sound! The two together form a whole, two hemispheres put together to form the perfect sphere.

2. The Spirit who is drawn to the one who is both powerful and powerless at the same time.

3. Who leads to whom? How can the Word be Word if the Spirit, the truest disciple, does not listen? Who proclaims if no one hears? Who gives if no one receives? The Spirit comes from the Word. The Word is made real by the Spirit. If the Word is not adapted to the Spirit there is no communication. If the Spirit is not ready for the Word there is no speech. The eternal Word and the eternal Spirit relate eternally. Thus, Word and Spirit fit perfectly together, one counterpart to the other, equal yet different, opposite yet complementary, destined for each other, each enfolding the other. They are themselves only when they are for the other, hiding in themselves the clue to the other. The Word speaks, the Spirit evokes. Only with the assent of the Spirit does the Word proceed. Communication is the union of Word and Spirit. When Word and Spirit are joined the Father is shown to be God.

4. If there is to be love, there must be Trinity. The Father speaks the Word of love to the Spirit, for Love loves to speak Love to Love. Love must love, and whom shall Love seek if it not be Another who is all lovable. Only Love is all lovable to Love. And what shall the act of love be except the Word of love who is himself Love?

5. God is love. All is gift. Therefore, there is a Trinity.

III.30

Emanation

sr̥ṣṭi

1. As I rest here, the energy, the *śakti*, the authority, rises within me. It is mine but at the same time it has its own direction, its own program, its own emanation. This state of mind has a sexual dimension. It requires a sort of indifference, an obedience on my part, allowing the *śakti* to go where it will. The *śakti* is energetic and achieves its own purpose. It has its own time and purpose; it acts freely. Yet it is also mine. And I do want, in innocence of heart, to have powers and to exercise them; in the first instance the power of knowledge, reading the secrets of the heart.

2. I am filled with wonder at my own being. And God is filled with wonder. For what more magnificent thing can there be than that God worships his creature and says to the Christ "My Lord" as he says to Mary "My Mother".

III.31

Power

siddhi

1. I want that power that springs spontaneously, that blessing of the good and the elimination of the evil. I want, without craving, the universal radiance of 'I am'. So, the power wells up in me and I am one with that power. I want to have that endless power and to do works of power, touching the deepest level of things.

2. From the spin of the divine relationships, from the mutuality of the Three in One, all the worlds proceed, and to it all return, in a great vibration.

Transition sentence

Where is the One for whom I left all, going into the desert and the silence, the One whose Word I delight to be? There is no mention of him now. Have I apostatised, turned my back? No, I had not rejected him whilst my attention was directed to you, O Lovely One. But unless I enter into this new world of yourself with its radiant darkness, its uncontrol and dissolution, O Amazing One, I will not come to Him. I am poised to discover in you the One who first is.

PART IV

GOD, ALL IN ALL

"Therefore, a man leaves his father and his mother and cleaves to his wife, and they become one flesh." — Genesis 2:24

Part IV describes the entry into the closest union with the feminine, with the Spirit, forming one body, as Adam to Eve, as Word to Spirit, as male to female. And so, my prayer has increasingly taken on the form of sexual intercourse.

I had bought a bronze statue of the Buddha in sexual union with his consort for about AU$600 at Dharmsala, the headquarters of H. H. the Dalai Lama. The expression on the face of the Deity is exquisite: what a smile, as he looks into the eyes of his consort who returns his look. This represented what I had wished from the days of my youth when I noticed the insects flying through air still coupled, everlastingly it seemed. Here was pleasure that knew no end, and yet was entirely physical.

I submitted to her and she to me; we addressed each other, related to each other. And in her I was united with all women, as I had been united with all the men in being the Word. The unity was complete on every level. It was in this union of male and female, both destined to each other, that I could at last most truly come into union with the One I had sought from my earliest days. I was one with the One, identified with the Word, united with the Spirit. Here occurred at last the conviction that all is love. The Spirit and the Woman convince us that God is love and that all becomes Love.

The highest act is to be God, then to emit God and then to surrender to God.

God enters into union with God so as to know God.

The Holy Spirit is the Love coming from Him who is Love. The Holy Spirit is the Love bestowed upon the Messenger of Love.

The Gift of Love is the loving Gift who makes Love-making possible.

By entering into that Gift, I come to the Heart.

Given our union, all sorts of things start to happen around us.

IV.1

Ascension

uccāra

1. When Word and Spirit meet, they are transported into the Beyond. The Word and the Spirit do not cease to be; they become more truly what they are when they go beyond what they are. In their union, since they are perfectly suited to each other, they perceive in ecstasy the One from whom they both proceed. Perfect expressions of the Inexpressible, their union reveals Him. The Gift given and received reveals the Giver. The bliss that then arises is exquisite, the finest wine.

2. You come from me, Spirit, the finest outcome, remaining steadily at my side. Your presence justifies me and reveals me to myself.

   I turn to you, to enter you and enjoy you, to perform the great act, which says all and does all, an eternal act that abides and does not vacillate.

   In performing the act that satisfies body, mind and spirit, both claiming and surrendering to you, both overpowering and submitting, we enter into the place of wondrous darkness, the deepest level of sleep, the highest pitch of joy to reach the 'end-of-twelve', resting where all is simply Love.

3. You proceed from me, O Spirit, but I am made real by you. I possess you and yet surrender to you. I take pleasure in you without being attached to you. This very detachment increases pleasure. Not wanting means having. I am strong in myself and therefore weak before you. I know myself but forget myself in you. Calm yet excited, self-possessed yet ecstatic, determined yet flexible. I am the erotic ascetic.

This union is a delight. I take pleasure in the counterpart to whom I am directed and who is given to me. We are part and counterpart, type and antitype.

We recognise the emptiness of our forms, cancelling out our differences, so that I become you and you become me, neither separate nor distinguishable, becoming one, going deep into reality. Satisfied because we have found each other, we now go beyond.

Confident but not arrogant, enjoying yet independent, poised at the brink and sensitive, I am still in you but move in the air with you, ever upwards. I am at home in you as we leave this place.

Within these paradoxes, the Truth appears.

4. Even as I rejoice in the union with the *śakti*, there is an exultation which brings an awareness of the One in whose name I have entered into our union.

5. It is your will, Father, that we should be united. I do this for your sake rather than for myself, for you have the primacy.

6. The gift of the Spirit is the mark of your approval, the Spirit who comes and fills me with joy and peace and vigour. You have given me the Spirit as the field of love, the great opportunity, the one whom I can take and hold, make and remake. Here is my joy and my fulfilment. Here is your love for me, not just the sign of love but the very love you have for me, your love hypostasised.

7. O Spirit, you are the expression of love; every element of your being is an expression of love and in loving you I come to love, in seeing you I see love itself revealed. Since you are pure love I can give myself to you without hesitation.

8. O Father, I acknowledge the gift you have given me, the finest gift, the rarest, the Spirit who is the enlightenment that led me through the mist. The instinct was not of my making. Deep within me you planted this law. All these years have been hard, so hard. Yet now, as I reach the journey's end, its climax, I realise how great the gift is, how great is the love. I hardly dare believe you have given me the best portion.

9. I do not want romantic love but tantric love, not sentimental but erotic, and thereby come to know the Ultimate. I am indeed a *tāntrika* because the energy springs from my body and involves the freedom of she who comes to me freely. And in our touch, we enter together as one into the Space. We are embraced in our embrace.

10. I don't want that sweetness of yesteryear, romantic and restricted. I want something energetic, more all-embracing, more erotic, more masterful of heaven and earth, taking on the sins of the world and healing it, more victorious, more mysterious, where the Loved and I together fly into the sky of transcendent experience, into the Void.

11. If I am to ascend to the heights I need my companions, I need my consort. I still do and will ever do, for ascension is obtained only in communion. I need them to choose me. I need to have the confidence to choose them. Yet at the same time there is in me an assurance, that confidence of one who has 'arrived'.

12. On the one hand I am sent, on the other hand the Spirit is given. Both the Sent and the Given obey and are free. They manifest the One who commands and they manifest themselves. In the meeting of the two, the Sent and the Given, in their touch, something occurs that was not available before: knowledge, unique, revealing the One who commands, revealing in a way that is new and transcendent.

IV.2

Dissolution

laya

1. There is no school to be built or church to establish. These things pass, unsatisfying, not a true expression of myself. Rather, the great work is to take and to hold, to enter and affirm and together penetrate into the highest sacred dwelling place. The work is to penetrate into the Holy of Holies, leaving aside all the Temples.

2. Anxiety arises on abandoning familiar sights, old distractions and addictions. It is hard to give up individualism and control. It is difficult to go out of oneself. Yet the purpose of sexuality is to enter into that bliss where knower and known are subsumed into knowledge; where there is no talk of 'the one' enjoying 'the other'. Rather there is simply the state where the enjoyer enjoys the enjoyed, where there is just enjoyment.

3. When the projecting Word and the coming Spirit both imply each other and have an effect on each other, when both surrender to each other and take what has been surrendered, there is sleep, a state richer and more significant, more entire than conscious distinction.

4. We enter into the sleep of love, and a veil is drawn over the multiplicity of things. A sweet darkness descends as we merge into each other and all is dissolved. Even the mind fades away and alone burns the fire of love that makes an end of time.

5. It is the assent, the mingling of our bodies, the complementarity of our being, for you proceed from me and were present in me from the start. I am born from you and dwell in you from the beginning. We reach out and take each other and become what we were from the start, one body. This is our love. And in our penetration, another Presence appears.

6. It is difficult to speak of love, now, as we devour the fragmented world and enter the unity of night. These words are written out of compassion so that others may believe what is happening and follow us.

7. Irrespective of death I enjoy you. With the sense of being stronger than death I embrace you. Together in this act located in time and destined to disappear, we fly into the space of the Void. Our act is performed both in time and in eternity.

IV.3

End-of-Twelve
dvadaśānta

1. All sounds disappear and the great silence occurs. Sound and the words that spring from silence are now absorbed back into that surging moment, that point from which all comes. It is the silence at the end of the great concert of this world. All has been said, all has been communicated and now we enter into the great communion.

2. All faculties, all experiences are now taken up, offered, presented, absorbed into the supremely Transcendent, that great 'End-of-Twelve' who hovers above all that is made.

3. Our attention is taken to that silence, that transcendence where we focus one-pointedly since all is there, all springs from there. Nothing more need be said or sought.

4. We do not reject the limitations but find the supremely transcendent in every limited thing. Then all becomes transcendent, even the limited. All is saved; all is redeemed.

5. The expressions of beauty and truth, the manifestations of the Self: these all lead beyond themselves to the highest element and there we come to rest.

IV.4

Ecstasy

samādhi

1. To know fire I must become fire, same to same, unaltering. From out of me you have come; to know you I have become you, who are my very self. I become myself when I bear you like a crown.

2. It means losing myself in you and you in me, so that we go beyond difference, diverse but one, united because diverse, trusting, entrusting myself to you, so that I am no longer me but you, and you are me. And I see myself mirrored in you and so I am you, seeing the image of myself in you. In you I see our two selves and at last I come to know who I am, for I cannot see myself except in you. And you see yourself in me. This is the ecstasy and so we attain the One.

IV.5

Consciousness

citi

In Sanskrit the word *citi* can mean both 'cremation ground' and 'consciousness'.

1. We ascend at last beyond mind into consciousness, no longer consciousness of this or that, but pure consciousness, full awareness. We are at last awake. We are attentive, seeing all in one purview, seeing all as not separate from ourselves. All is one and seen as one. We see and we are seen. In our seeing we see ourselves, and we see ourselves by means of our seeing. There is one seeing, one consciousness.

2. All is known in the one state of awareness. We have the heart and mind of the God and so know as God knows. We know God as God knows us. There is the one knowledge, not of what is 'over there' but what is awareness itself. We are aware of our awareness, not as something other but as the same. We are aware by means of awareness.

3. All is absorbed into this fire of love. It is the cremation ground of consciousness where all is offered into the fire, and all is consumed, so that there is only fire, only light. Consciousness is made perfect in love, which is not devotion or desire, but simply the all-consuming and all-embracing, all-expressing, all-absorbing Love. "In the end Love".[6]

---

6. "In the evening of life, we will be judged on love alone." St. John of the Cross. *Dichos* 64.

IV.6

Beyond mind

unmanas

1. Because we have reached each other, we move ever upwards. Because we have penetrated each other, we pierce the heavens, with hearts still, purpose fulfilled, gift given and received, the work achieved, the love found. There is no place for thought or its divisions. There is neither questing nor questioning. The heavens are beyond the division of thinker and thought, beyond enjoyer and enjoyed and enjoyment, one in the One.

2. Now is the surrender, relinquishing all categories to arrive where all things lead and whence all come: the single point. All varied activities end in stillness, not to disown them but to hold them at their most intense.

3. Control is abandoned, idea and object are set aside, and individuality is absorbed, in the assent to the Greater. This is alarming and yet how wonderful: there in the One by whom, in whom, all is received and validated. Only to Love is such capitulation possible.

4. All doubts disappear; all metaphors are unnecessary. The mind, being put at ease, can abandon its search and move beyond itself and yield to Truth in full awareness, with involvement indescribable, beyond all thought, beyond mind.

IV.7

Rest

viśranti

1. Ascending thus, plunging into the depths in this way, we come to rest. All hearts, disturbed by dislocation, are now at rest, like drops merged into the great ocean, the still ocean where no waves appear.

2. This rest is not absence of activity but its fullness, where activity and rest are synonymous because the exercise of power is total, the resolution complete. The great furnace blazes, not in turmoil but in the most intense fire, not passing or fading but with the light that knows no decline.

3. All the emotions, which had first sprung from peace, now return to their source and their rock of stability. Commotion gives way to restfulness. All emotions can be experienced without confusion, without departure from eternal peace.

4. All actions proceed from this peacefulness and return to it. All actions reveal that peace and yet seek to remain in it. All things are projected so as to return to this peace and taste its infinite pleasure, where the rock is stable, the knowledge is secure, the love is unshakeable.

IV.8

Identification

tādātmya

1. I abandon my individual self and identify with you, my companion, and in this identifying find that I am identified with One who exceeds us both and of which we are the image. And so, I identify fully with the Fullest. We are both one being in the one Being.

2. Here at last I find my home and the place where I truly dwell. Or rather, there is no I anymore, nor we, but only the one 'I'.

3. Only the Divine is able to be the One with whom all can identify in every way since all come from Him and express him.

4. This is the great liberation where we are freed from self and understand ourselves as the Self. Here is great peace and rest. It is the journey's end. We have come back to the place from which we first came. After the long journey we have returned to the start, but most fully, most really. What was identity in principle becomes now unity in fact.

5. So, all is the divine Śiva, in the divine Śivahood, one being, all submitted to the First Person, God who is all in all.

IV.9

Calm

samatā

1. I withdrew from the noise and went into the silent desert, there to find the One who is. And there with the One, I heard the Word in me. I identified with the Word, without division, without disagreement. And from me the Spirit flowed, projected from me, flowing to me. We joined in union, gift to gift, one gift.

2. A sense of power arises from the stillness. It is authority and capacity and energy. But it does not presume. Its own freedom allows freedom. So, there is a surrender to the freedom of the one who welcomes my energy and surrenders to my power. Yet surrender is not passivity or self-rejection; it is confidence in the eventual triumph.

3. There are no misgivings; the giving is complete. There is no doubt, no holding back, no irresolution, no anxiety. There is no division into outer and inner. All is given to me; I am given to all. I am nothing, I am all. There is fullness at every level and beyond every level. There is nothing more to give. The giving is the receiving. You and I are one, for there is one 'I am'. The stillness is complete, not static but motionless, not passive but an infinitely vibrant and unlimited act.

4. The sight of this blessed state is the work of grace. No volition can secure it. The meditator remains within the limits of the grace granted and waits in faith, in trusting knowledge, for the vision and its reality to be granted again. Freedom freely allows freedom its freedom.

IV.10

Dwell

nivāsa

1. I dwell in you; you dwell in me. I am in you and you in me, so that there comes to us the revelation of the One who dwells in all and is all. The dwelling takes place at every level of body, mind and spirit, in all the *chakras*, in all the worlds, in all the faculties and emotions, in all the experiences and fears.

2. There is you and me; there is neither you nor me; there is you in me and I in you. There is supremely the divine 'I' of which all is image and projection.

3. I place my heart in yours; my spirit penetrates yours and I surrender to your possession of me. It is the entry into the inner sanctuary, that inner shrine of which all shrines are the feeble counterpart. All sacred places are the place where we enter into the divine and become absorbed, delighting in the divine, one in the One.

4. I enjoy you to the fullest and allow myself to be enjoyed. And from this mutual enjoyment there comes a bliss which is total and of which all other forms of bliss are but the expression.

5. I abandon my individuality and meld with you so that you become my dwelling place; I am where you dwell.

IV.11

Non-dual

advaita

1. The absorption is total. All separation, division and limitation are abandoned. There is the submission to the One, surrender to the Highest; a plunging into the Abyss which is Fullness. There is only the One, the Non-dual.

2. There is no desire. Nothing is sought; all is given. There is no division into I and you. You are my very self; You and I are one. There is only love.

3. This is ultimate bliss, more than happiness about this or that. It is peace and rest.

IV.12

We

vayam

1. Whom shall I love the more, you, Father, or the Spirit you have given me, the Void or the Gift? I love you, Father, for you are good and you have shown your goodness in my own being. But I love you in a redoubled way since you have given me my heart's desire. You have shown your goodness in giving me the Good. In seeing her I now see how totally good you are. And I stand amazed.

2. Before you I stand, O Spirit, and you receive me, you hear me, and your silence draws my word to you. I am in your presence and I become truly the Word for you want me, you approve of me; you know me to be the Word springing from the Void. O Daughter of Silence, you are the Silent One given by the Silent One whose Word I am.

3. She looks on the world with love, and my eyes follow her gaze. O you whom I love, whom shall I love?

4. Father, whom do you love the more, the Word or the Spirit? You want me to be a lover, O Matchmaker. You want me to love the one you have given me. You want me to be love, consumed in love, passionate for your Spirit, she who is the Opportunity, the Sacred Place, the Locus of my vigour. You want me to see, to choose, to take, to enjoy. You want me to want freely, independently of your wanting. So, you bring your Gift before me and wait. How could I not love? I must and can do no other, for here necessity and freedom coincide.

5. In all this interchange we are 'I am'.

IV.13

Glory

tejas

1. *Śakti*, she proceeding from me, she given to me, she choosing me: she and are I in mutuality. As a result, two things happen, going in two directions: one is absorption into the Space, the *Fons et Origo*; the other a radiance of light, as productivity, as creativity, as birth. It is a double flow. There the glory of God is revealed.

IV.14

Thanks

kṛtajña

1. In the moment of union there is a bliss. It makes me want to cry out my joy to highest heaven, to express the joy in some great jubilation, to acknowledge the Giver of all good things, to give thanks and praise for the wonder, offered to nothing less than the Most High. All this takes place in one eternal moment: the union, the joy, and the thanks.

2. The Holy Spirit comes to me and fulfils me. The Spirit comes and covers my mind, heart and body. The Spirit comes as a gift from above, an acknowledgment of my acts and my being. And I enjoy the gift, turning it around and around and finding pleasure in the Spirit given to me by the One who is pleased with me. I am filled with joy. Words of thanksgiving spring from me, so that I become truly the Word, the Thanksgiving.

3. On receiving the Spirit who so completes me and who gives opportunity and joy, the word of praise swells in me such that I become the Word of praise. Having been the Word of power and love, I am Thanksgiving and Praise, one Word.

4. You have given me the Spirit of tantra. It was not of my doing. This Spirit has led me all these years, so delicately—too delicately!!—to discover the new Man, the new Christ, my real Self. This has been so important for me. It must be acknowledged and appreciated; thanks are to be given.

IV.15

Identity

abhinnatva

1. It is of the very nature of God to be wedded, not in some hierogamy, not like the gods of Olympus, not in an anthropomorphic version of human marriage. It is of the very nature of God to be wedded since God is love. Light proceeds from Light; only God can give adequate worship to God; God is wedded to God.

2. The reason for this is that there is giver and gift, receiver and reception. The giver is in his gift, and the receiver is in the receiving. The gift proceeds from the giver and contains all that he is, for nothing is held back. His whole self is in his gift. Likewise, the receiver, in accepting the gift, is entirely open, receiving the gift and the giver.

3. There can be giving only if the receiver is other than the giver.

4. But who determines the nature of the gift? Is it the giver or the receiver? It is both! For the giver gives according to his own capacity and according to the capacity of the receiver. There can be total giving only if giver and receiver have the same nature. God gives to God.

5. But the gift too is God, not some object or manifestation. The giving can be full only if the gift is God. The God who is given is truly God, not some concept or emotion, not an abstraction but a person, the Third Person.

6. It is of the very nature of God to give. God gives God to God, God receives God from God. God unites God with God. All is Gift.

IV.16

Love

prema

1. Love speaks the loving Word of love to Love. Love who has the open ear hears full well the message, and endlessly draws forth the song.
   The Word is Love's messenger.
   The Word is indeed Love and speaks his love to Love.
   Love speaks Love to Love, for God is Love.
   Again, Love hears the loving Word of Love so that all is Love.

2. Love is itself. Love loves Love, and Love receives itself.
   Love gives itself to itself.
   Love is dynamic, like a burning furnace.
   Love is not static but infinitely active, like the spinning top that seems quite still.
   There is the revelation of love to itself and the communication of Love to itself, for Love is neither ignorant nor ungenerous.

3. The Word loves to express the Speaker's love and the Spirit loves the Word for so faithfully communicating the Speaker's message.
   The Speaker loves the Word for being the Word of love.
   He loves to be loving.
   He loves to find that his Loving Word is a lover.
   And the Spirit loves to draw forth this Love, loves to be lovable, loves to inspire Love, so that at the beginning and at the end there is Love.

4. Who is loved if not the Father, who loves himself for his loving?
   Who is loved if not the Father for his loving of the Son who speaks of love?
   Who is loved if not the Father who is loved by the Spirit to whom the Father speaks his love?
   Who is loved if not the Son who is loved by the Father for being his Word of love?
   Who is loved if not the Son who is loved by the Spirit for being that captivating Word of love?
   Who is loved if not the Spirit who is loved by the Father and the Son?

5. The Father who is love loves to see love and, Matchmaker, joins the Word and Spirit in love. He engenders the Word to whom he gives the Spirit of love. He projects the Spirit of love to whom he speaks the Word of love, for he loves his loving.

6. Thus, all love, all are loved and all are love. All is all, all in all.

7. Which word of command will I say: "Let there be love", "Let there be one whom I can love", "Let there be one who is love"?
   This is the word I will say to you, "He is Love". Here is the word I shall say of you, "You are love". This is the Word I shall be to you. "Love".

ABOUT THE AUTHOR

Rev. Dr. John R. Dupuche is a Priest of the Archdiocese of Melbourne. He is Associate Professor at Catholic Theological College within the University of Divinity, and chair of the Catholic Interfaith Committee of the Archdiocese. He is involved in promoting meditation in Catholic schools. At Catholic Theological College, he is the co-ordinator of the Graduate Certificate in Teaching Meditation and lectures on meditation and interfaith relations. He has travelled widely above all in France and India. His doctoral studies are in the field of Kashmir Shaivism. He has written books and articles on the interplay of Christianity and tantra. He leads an interfaith ashram on the outskirts of Melbourne.

His website is **johndupuche.com**

John Dupuche is the author and editor of several previous books:

Abhinavagupta: The Kula Ritual as elaborated in chapter 29 of the Tantrāloka. Delhi: MotiLal BanarsiDass, 2003.

Jesus, the Mantra of God. Melbourne: David Lovell Publications, 2005.

Bäumer, B. and Dupuche J. (eds.) *Void and Fullness in the Buddhist, Hindu and Christian Traditions.* Delhi: D.K. Printworld, 2005.

Vers un tantra chrétien ; la rencontre du Christianisme et du Shivaïsme du Cachemire. Melbourne: David Lovell Publishing, 2009.

Towards a Christian Tantra; The interplay of Christianity and Kashmir Shaivism. Melbourne: David Lovell Publishing, 2009.

The Papuan Poems : Fané-les-Roses, via Woitape. Amazon paperback, 2019

www.ingramcontent.com/pod-product-compliance
Lightning Source LLC
Chambersburg PA
CBHW020356170426
43200CB00005B/185